Writings of Kahlil Gibran

The Prophet, The Madman, The Wanderer, and Others

by Kahlil Gibran

Introduction by Lenny Flank

Red and Black Publishers, St Petersburg, Florida

Contents

Introduction

Gibran Kahlil Gibran was born in January 1883 to a poor family in the town of Bsharri in northern Lebanon. His mother, Kamila, was the daughter of a Maronite Catholic priest and imbued her children with a strong religious spirit. As a young boy, Gibran spent much time alone in the mountains and forests around Bsharri. Although he never went to school, Gibran was taught to read and write by the local Catholic priests. As a young boy he accidentally fell off a cliff and injured his shoulder, and spent the next 40 days with his arm strapped to his chest. Gibran's childhood gave him a deep reverence for nature and a long-lasting spiritualistic view that was independent of church doctrine.

When Gibran was eight years old, his father, a local government official, was arrested for embezzlement and the family's house was confiscated by the authorities. Kamali took her son and two daughters and emigrated to the US, arriving in 1895. They settled first in New York

City, then in the large Syrian/Lebanese community in Boston's South End.

For the first time, Gibran got the opportunity to go to school. Through his teachers, he became active in the Boston art community, and became a protege of local artist Fred Holland Day. An accomplished artist, Gibran did covers for a number of books before trying his hand at writing. At the age of 15, Gibran returned to Lebanon to attend an art school in Beirut, where he helped found a student literary magazine. Returning to the US in 1902, he had his first art exhibit in Boston two years later, then went to Paris to study art until 1910.

On his return to the US, Gibran moved to New York and began a series of writings, originally in Arabic, which took for the form of short allegories and verse that were heavily influenced by his childhood love for nature and by religious spiritualism, particularly by Maronite Christianity and Islamic Sufi traditions. His first work in English, "The Madman", was published in 1918. His most famous work, "The Prophet", was published in 1923.

Gibran died in April 1931, of tuberculosis, at the age of 48. Although he had lived in the US for most of his adult life, he had never become a US citizen, and wanted to be buries in his native Lebanon. His grave is at the Mar Sarkis monastery in his home town of Bsharri, which is now the Gibran Museum.

The peak of Kahlil Gibran's popularity came decades after his death, when the counterculture movement of the 1960's adopted his spiritual mysticism. "The Prophet" was translated into over 40 languages, and has never been out of print. Gibran is now the third best-selling poet of all time, behind only Lao-Tzu and Shakespeare.

The Prophet

1923

The Coming of The Ship

Almustafa, the chosen and the beloved, who was a dawn onto his own day, had waited twelve years in the city of Orphalese for his ship that was to return and bear him back to the isle of his birth.

And in the twelfth year, on the seventh day of Ielool, the month of reaping, he climbed the hill without the city walls and looked seaward; and he beheld the ship coming with the mist.

Then the gates of his heart were flung open, and his joy flew far over the sea. And he closed his eyes and prayed in the silences of his soul.

But he descended the hill, a sadness came upon him, and he thought in his heart: How shall I go in peace and without sorrow? Nay, not without a wound in the spirit shall I leave this city.

Long were the days of pain I have spent within its walls, and long were the nights of aloneness; and who can depart from his pain and his aloneness without regret?

Too many fragments of the spirit have I scattered in these streets, and too many are the children of my longing that walk naked among these hills, and I cannot withdraw from them without a burden and an ache.

It is not a garment I cast off this day, but a skin that I tear with my own hands.

Nor is it a thought I leave behind me, but a heart made sweet with hunger and with thirst.

Yet I cannot tarry longer.

The sea that calls all things unto her calls me, and I must embark.

For to stay, though the hours burn in the night, is to freeze and crystallize and be bound in a mould.

Fain would I take with me all that is here. But how shall I?

A voice cannot carry the tongue and the lips that give it wings. Alone must it seek the ether.

And alone and without his nest shall the eagle fly across the sun.

Now when he reached the foot of the hill, he turned again towards the sea, and he saw his ship approaching the harbor, and upon her prow the mariners, the men of his own land.

And his soul cried out to them, and he said:

Sons of my ancient mother, you riders of the tides, How often have you sailed in my dreams. And now you come in my awakening, which is my deeper dream.

Ready am I to go, and my eagerness with sails full set awaits the wind.

Only another breath will I breathe in this still air, only another loving look cast backward,

Then I shall stand among you, a seafarer among seafarers.

And you, vast sea, sleepless mother,

Who alone are peace and freedom to the river and the stream,

Only another winding will this stream make, only another murmur in this glade,

And then shall I come to you, a boundless drop to a boundless ocean.

And as he walked he saw from afar men and women leaving their fields and their vineyards and hastening towards the city gates.

And he heard their voices calling his name, and shouting from the field to field telling one another of the coming of the ship.

And he said to himself:

Shall the day of parting be the day of gathering?

And shall it be said that my eve was in truth my dawn?

And what shall I give unto him who has left his plough in midfurrow, or to him who has stopped the wheel of his winepress?

Shall my heart become a tree heavy-laden with fruit that I may gather and give unto them?

And shall my desires flow like a fountain that I may fill their cups?

Am I a harp that the hand of the mighty may touch me, or a flute that his breath may pass through me?

A seeker of silences am I, and what treasure have I found in silences that I may dispense with confidence?

If this is my day of harvest, in what fields have I sowed the seed, and in what unremembered seasons?

If this indeed be the hour in which I lift up my lantern, it is not my flame that shall burn therein.

Empty and dark shall I raise my lantern,

And the guardian of the night shall fill it with oil and he shall light it also.

These things he said in words. But much in his heart remained unsaid. For he himself could not speak his deeper secret.

And when he entered into the city all the people came to meet him, and they were crying out to him as with one voice.

And the elders of the city stood forth and said:

Go not yet away from us.

A noontide have you been in our twilight, and your youth has given us dreams to dream.

No stranger are you among us, nor a guest, but our son and our dearly beloved.

Suffer not yet our eyes to hunger for your face.

And the priests and the priestesses said unto him:

Let not the waves of the sea separate us now, and the years you have spent in our midst become a memory.

You have walked among us a spirit, and your shadow has been a light upon our faces.

Much have we loved you. But speechless was our love, and with veils has it been veiled.

Yet now it cries aloud unto you, and would stand revealed before you.

And ever has it been that love knows not its own depth until the hour of separation.

And others came also and entreated him.

But he answered them not. He only bent his head; and those who stood near saw his tears falling upon his breast.

And he and the people proceeded towards the great square before the temple.

And there came out of the sanctuary a woman whose name was Almitra. And she was a seeress.

And he looked upon her with exceeding tenderness, for it was she who had first sought and believed in him when he had been but a day in their city.

And she hailed him, saying:

Prophet of God, in quest for the uttermost, long have you searched the distances for your ship.

And now your ship has come, and you must needs go.

Deep is your longing for the land of your memories and the dwelling place of your greater desires; and our love would not bind you nor our needs hold you.

Yet this we ask ere you leave us, that you speak to us and give us of your truth.

And we will give it unto our children, and they unto their children, and it shall not perish.

In your aloneness you have watched with our days, and in your wakefulness you have listened to the weeping and the laughter of our sleep.

Now therefore disclose us to ourselves, and tell us all that has been shown you of that which is between birth and death.

And he answered,

People of Orphalese, of what can I speak save of that which is even now moving your souls?

Love

Then said Almitra, "Speak to us of Love."

And he raised his head and looked upon the people, and there fell a stillness upon them.

And with a great voice he said:

When love beckons to you follow him,

Though his ways are hard and steep.

And when his wings enfold you yield to him,

Though the sword hidden among his pinions may wound you.

And when he speaks to you believe in him,

Though his voice may shatter your dreams as the north wind lays waste the garden.

For even as love crowns you so shall he crucify you. Even as he is for your growth so is he for your pruning.

Even as he ascends to your height and caresses your tenderest branches that quiver in the sun,

So shall he descend to your roots and shake them in their clinging to the earth.

Like sheaves of corn he gathers you unto himself.

He threshes you to make you naked.

He sifts you to free you from your husks.

He grinds you to whiteness.

He kneads you until you are pliant;

And then he assigns you to his sacred fire, that you may become sacred bread for God's sacred feast.

All these things shall love do unto you that you may know the secrets of your heart, and in that knowledge become a fragment of Life's heart.

But if in your fear you would seek only love's peace and love's pleasure,

Then it is better for you that you cover your nakedness and pass out of love's threshing-floor,

Into the seasonless world where you shall laugh, but not all of your laughter, and weep, but not all of your tears.

Love gives naught but itself and takes naught but from itself.

Love possesses not nor would it be possessed;

For love is sufficient unto love.

When you love you should not say, "God is in my heart," but rather, I am in the heart of God."

And think not you can direct the course of love; if it finds you worthy, it directs your course.

Love has no other desire but to fulfil itself.

But if you love and must needs have desires, let these be your desires:

To melt and be like a running brook that sings its melody to the night.

To know the pain of too much tenderness.

To be wounded by your own understanding of love;

And to bleed willingly and joyfully.

To wake at dawn with a winged heart and give thanks for another day of loving;

To rest at the noon hour and meditate love's ecstasy;

To return home at eventide with gratitude;

And then to sleep with a prayer for the beloved in your heart and a song of praise upon your lips.

Marriage

Then Almitra spoke again and said, "And what of Marriage, master?"

And he answered saying:

You were born together, and together you shall be forevermore.

You shall be together when white wings of death scatter your days.

Aye, you shall be together even in the silent memory of God.

But let there be spaces in your togetherness,

And let the winds of the heavens dance between you.

Love one another but make not a bond of love:

Let it rather be a moving sea between the shores of your souls.

Fill each other's cup but drink not from one cup.

Give one another of your bread but eat not from the same loaf.

Sing and dance together and be joyous, but let each one of you be alone,

Even as the strings of a lute are alone though they quiver with the same music.

Give your hearts, but not into each other's keeping.

For only the hand of Life can contain your hearts.

And stand together, yet not too near together:

For the pillars of the temple stand apart,

And the oak tree and the cypress grow not in each other's shadow.

Children

And a woman who held a babe against her bosom said, "Speak to us of Children."

And he said:

Your children are not your children.

They are the sons and daughters of Life's longing for itself.

They come through you but not from you,

And though they are with you, yet they belong not to you.

You may give them your love but not your thoughts.

For they have their own thoughts.

You may house their bodies but not their souls,

For their souls dwell in the house of tomorrow, which you cannot visit, not even in your dreams.

You may strive to be like them, but seek not to make them like you.

For life goes not backward nor tarries with yesterday.

You are the bows from which your children as living arrows are sent forth.

The archer sees the mark upon the path of the infinite, and He bends you with His might that His arrows may go swift and far.

Let your bending in the archer's hand be for gladness;

For even as he loves the arrow that flies, so He loves also the bow that is stable.

Giving

Then said a rich man, "Speak to us of Giving."

And he answered:

You give but little when you give of your possessions.

It is when you give of yourself that you truly give.

For what are your possessions but things you keep and guard for fear you may need them tomorrow?

And tomorrow, what shall tomorrow bring to the overprudent dog burying bones in the trackless sand as he follows the pilgrims to the holy city?

And what is fear of need but need itself?

Is not dread of thirst when your well is full, thirst that is unquenchable?

There are those who give little of the much which they have - and they give it for recognition and their hidden desire makes their gifts unwholesome.

And there are those who have little and give it all.

These are the believers in life and the bounty of life, and their coffer is never empty.

There are those who give with joy, and that joy is their reward.

And there are those who give with pain, and that pain is their baptism.

And there are those who give and know not pain in giving, nor do they seek joy, nor give with mindfulness of virtue;

They give as in yonder valley the myrtle breathes its fragrance into space.

Though the hands of such as these God speaks, and from behind their eyes He smiles upon the earth.

It is well to give when asked, but it is better to give unasked, through understanding;

And to the open-handed the search for one who shall receive is joy greater than giving

And is there aught you would withhold?

All you have shall some day be given;

Therefore give now, that the season of giving may be yours and not your inheritors'.

You often say, "I would give, but only to the deserving."

The trees in your orchard say not so, nor the flocks in your pasture.

They give that they may live, for to withhold is to perish.

Surely he who is worthy to receive his days and his nights is worthy of all else from you.

And he who has deserved to drink from the ocean of life deserves to fill his cup from your little stream.

And what desert greater shall there be than that which lies in the courage and the confidence, nay the charity, of receiving?

And who are you that men should rend their bosom and unveil their pride, that you may see their worth naked and their pride unabashed?

See first that you yourself deserve to be a giver, and an instrument of giving.

For in truth it is life that gives unto life - while you, who deem yourself a giver, are but a witness.

And you receivers - and you are all receivers - assume no weight of gratitude, lest you lay a yoke upon yourself and upon him who gives.

Rather rise together with the giver on his gifts as on wings;

For to be overmindful of your debt, is to doubt his generosity who has the free-hearted earth for mother, and God for father.

Eating And Drinking

Then an old man, a keeper of an inn, said, "Speak to us of Eating and Drinking."

And he said:

Would that you could live on the fragrance of the earth, and like an air plant be sustained by the light.

But since you must kill to eat, and rob the young of its mother's milk to quench your thirst, let it then be an act of worship,

And let your board stand an altar on which the pure and the innocent of forest and plain are sacrificed for that which is purer and still more innocent in many.

When you kill a beast say to him in your heart,

"By the same power that slays you, I to am slain; and I too shall be consumed. For the law that delivered you into my hand shall deliver me into a mightier hand.

Your blood and my blood is naught but the sap that feeds the tree of heaven."

And when you crush an apple with your teeth, say to it in your heart,

"Your seeds shall live in my body,

And the buds of your tomorrow shall blossom in my heart,

And your fragrance shall be my breath,

And together we shall rejoice through all the seasons."

And in the autumn, when you gather the grapes of your vineyard for the winepress, say in you heart,

"I too am a vineyard, and my fruit shall be gathered for the winepress,

And like new wine I shall be kept in eternal vessels."

And in winter, when you draw the wine, let there be in your heart a song for each cup;

And let there be in the song a remembrance for the autumn days, and for the vineyard, and for the winepress.

Work

Then a ploughman said, "Speak to us of Work."

And he answered, saying:

You work that you may keep pace with the earth and the soul of the earth.

For to be idle is to become a stranger unto the seasons, and to step out of life's procession, that marches in majesty and proud submission towards the infinite.

When you work you are a flute through whose heart the whispering of the hours turns to music.

Which of you would be a reed, dumb and silent, when all else sings together in unison?

Always you have been told that work is a curse and labor a misfortune.

But I say to you that when you work you fulfil a part of earth's furthest dream, assigned to you when that dream was born,

And in keeping yourself with labor you are in truth loving life,

And to love life through labor is to be intimate with life's inmost secret.

But if you in your pain call birth an affliction and the support of the flesh a curse written upon your brow, then I answer that naught but the sweat of your brow shall wash away that which is written.

You have been told also life is darkness, and in your weariness you echo what was said by the weary.

And I say that life is indeed darkness save when there is urge,

And all urge is blind save when there is knowledge,

And all knowledge is vain save when there is work,

And all work is empty save when there is love;

And when you work with love you bind yourself to yourself, and to one another, and to God.

And what is it to work with love?

It is to weave the cloth with threads drawn from your heart, even as if your beloved were to wear that cloth.

It is to build a house with affection, even as if your beloved were to dwell in that house.

It is to sow seeds with tenderness and reap the harvest with joy, even as if your beloved were to eat the fruit.

It is to charge all things you fashion with a breath of your own spirit,

And to know that all the blessed dead are standing about you and watching.

Often have I heard you say, as if speaking in sleep, "he who works in marble, and finds the shape of his own soul in the stone, is a nobler than he who ploughs the soil.

And he who seizes the rainbow to lay it on a cloth in the likeness of man, is more than he who makes the sandals for our feet."

But I say, not in sleep but in the over-wakefulness of noontide, that the wind speaks not more sweetly to the giant oaks than to the least of all the blades of grass;

And he alone is great who turns the voice of the wind into a song made sweeter by his own loving.

Work is love made visible.

And if you cannot work with love but only with distaste, it is better that you should leave your work and sit at the gate of the temple and take alms of those who work with joy.

For if you bake bread with indifference, you bake a bitter bread that feeds but half man's hunger.

And if you grudge the crushing of the grapes, your grudge distils a poison in the wine.

And if you sing though as angels, and love not the singing, you muffle man's ears to the voices of the day and the voices of the night.

Joy And Sorrow

Then a woman said, "Speak to us of Joy and Sorrow."
And he answered:
Your joy is your sorrow unmasked.

And the selfsame well from which your laughter rises was oftentimes filled with your tears.

And how else can it be?

The deeper that sorrow carves into your being, the more joy you can contain.

Is not the cup that hold your wine the very cup that was burned in the potter's oven?

And is not the lute that soothes your spirit, the very wood that was hollowed with knives?

When you are joyous, look deep into your heart and you shall find it is only that which has given you sorrow that is giving you joy.

When you are sorrowful look again in your heart, and you shall see that in truth you are weeping for that which has been your delight.

Some of you say, "Joy is greater than sorrow," and others say, "Nay, sorrow is the greater."

But I say unto you, they are inseparable.

Together they come, and when one sits alone with you at your board, remember that the other is asleep upon your bed.

Verily you are suspended like scales between your sorrow and your joy.

Only when you are empty are you at standstill and balanced.

When the treasure-keeper lifts you to weigh his gold and his silver, needs must your joy or your sorrow rise or fall.

Houses

A mason came forth and said, "Speak to us of Houses."

And he answered and said:

Build of your imaginings a bower in the wilderness ere you build a house within the city walls.

For even as you have home-comings in your twilight, so has the wanderer in you, the ever distant and alone.

Your house is your larger body.

It grows in the sun and sleeps in the stillness of the night; and it is not dreamless.

Does not your house dream? And dreaming, leave the city for grove or hilltop?

Would that I could gather your houses into my hand, and like a sower scatter them in forest and meadow.

Would the valleys were your streets, and the green paths your alleys, that you might seek one another through vineyards, and come with the fragrance of the earth in your garments.

But these things are not yet to be.

In their fear your forefathers gathered you too near together. And that fear shall endure a little longer. A little longer shall your city walls separate your hearths from your fields.

And tell me, people of Orphalese, what have you in these houses? And what is it you guard with fastened doors?

Have you peace, the quiet urge that reveals your power?

Have you remembrances, the glimmering arches that span the summits of the mind?

Have you beauty, that leads the heart from things fashioned of wood and stone to the holy mountain?

Tell me, have you these in your houses?

Or have you only comfort, and the lust for comfort, that stealthy thing that enters the house a guest, and becomes a host, and then a master?

Ay, and it becomes a tamer, and with hook and scourge makes puppets of your larger desires.

Though its hands are silken, its heart is of iron.

It lulls you to sleep only to stand by your bed and jeer at the dignity of the flesh.

It makes mock of your sound senses, and lays them in thistledown like fragile vessels.

Verily the lust for comfort murders the passion of the soul, and then walks grinning in the funeral.

But you, children of space, you restless in rest, you shall not be trapped nor tamed.

Your house shall be not an anchor but a mast.

It shall not be a glistening film that covers a wound, but an eyelid that guards the eye.

You shall not fold your wings that you may pass through doors, nor bend your heads that they strike not against a ceiling, nor fear to breathe lest walls should crack and fall down.

You shall not dwell in tombs made by the dead for the living.

And though of magnificence and splendor, your house shall not hold your secret nor shelter your longing.

For that which is boundless in you abides in the mansion of the sky, whose door is the morning mist, and whose windows are the songs and the silences of night.

Clothes

And the weaver said, "Speak to us of Clothes."

And he answered:

Your clothes conceal much of your beauty, yet they hide not the unbeautiful.

And though you seek in garments the freedom of privacy you may find in them a harness and a chain.

Would that you could meet the sun and the wind with more of your skin and less of your raiment,

For the breath of life is in the sunlight and the hand of life is in the wind.

Some of you say, "It is the north wind who has woven the clothes to wear."

But shame was his loom, and the softening of the sinews was his thread.

And when his work was done he laughed in the forest.

Forget not that modesty is for a shield against the eye of the unclean.

And when the unclean shall be no more, what were modesty but a fetter and a fouling of the mind?

And forget not that the earth delights to feel your bare feet and the winds long to play with your hair.

Buying And Selling

And a merchant said, "Speak to us of Buying and Selling."

And he answered and said:

To you the earth yields her fruit, and you shall not want if you but know how to fill your hands.

It is in exchanging the gifts of the earth that you shall find abundance and be satisfied.

Yet unless the exchange be in love and kindly justice, it will but lead some to greed and others to hunger.

When in the market place you toilers of the sea and fields and vineyards meet the weavers and the potters and the gatherers of spices,

Invoke then the master spirit of the earth, to come into your midst and sanctify the scales and the reckoning that weighs value against value.

And suffer not the barren-handed to take part in your transactions, who would sell their words for your labor.

To such men you should say,

"Come with us to the field, or go with our brothers to the sea and cast your net;

For the land and the sea shall be bountiful to you even as to us."

And if there come the singers and the dancers and the flute players - buy of their gifts also.

For they too are gatherers of fruit and frankincense, and that which they bring, though fashioned of dreams, is raiment and food for your soul.

And before you leave the marketplace, see that no one has gone his way with empty hands.

For the master spirit of the earth shall not sleep peacefully upon the wind till the needs of the least of you are satisfied.

Crime And Punishment

Then one of the judges of the city stood forth and said, "Speak to us of Crime and Punishment."

And he answered saying:

It is when your spirit goes wandering upon the wind,

That you, alone and unguarded, commit a wrong unto others and therefore unto yourself.

And for that wrong committed must you knock and wait a while unheeded at the gate of the blessed.

Like the ocean is your god-self;

It remains for ever undefiled.

And like the ether it lifts but the winged.

Even like the sun is your god-self;

It knows not the ways of the mole nor seeks it the holes of the serpent.

But your god-self does not dwell alone in your being.

Much in you is still man, and much in you is not yet man,

But a shapeless pigmy that walks asleep in the mist searching for its own awakening.

And of the man in you would I now speak.

For it is he and not your god-self nor the pigmy in the mist, that knows crime and the punishment of crime.

Oftentimes have I heard you speak of one who commits a wrong as though he were not one of you, but a stranger unto you and an intruder upon your world.

But I say that even as the holy and the righteous cannot rise beyond the highest which is in each one of you,

So the wicked and the weak cannot fall lower than the lowest which is in you also.

And as a single leaf turns not yellow but with the silent knowledge of the whole tree,

So the wrong-doer cannot do wrong without the hidden will of you all.

Like a procession you walk together towards your god-self.

You are the way and the wayfarers.

And when one of you falls down he falls for those behind him, a caution against the stumbling stone.

Ay, and he falls for those ahead of him, who though faster and surer of foot, yet removed not the stumbling stone.

And this also, though the word lie heavy upon your hearts:

The murdered is not unaccountable for his own murder,

And the robbed is not blameless in being robbed.

The righteous is not innocent of the deeds of the wicked,

And the white-handed is not clean in the doings of the felon.

Yea, the guilty is oftentimes the victim of the injured,

And still more often the condemned is the burden-bearer for the guiltless and unblamed.

You cannot separate the just from the unjust and the good from the wicked;

For they stand together before the face of the sun even as the black thread and the white are woven together.

And when the black thread breaks, the weaver shall look into the whole cloth, and he shall examine the loom also.

If any of you would bring judgment on the unfaithful wife,

Let him also weight the heart of her husband in scales, and measure his soul with measurements.

And let him who would lash the offender look unto the spirit of the offended.

And if any of you would punish in the name of righteousness and lay the ax unto the evil tree, let him see to its roots;

And verily he will find the roots of the good and the bad, the fruitful and the fruitless, all entwined together in the silent heart of the earth.

And you judges who would be just,

What judgment pronounce you upon him who though honest in the flesh yet is a thief in spirit?

What penalty lay you upon him who slays in the flesh yet is himself slain in the spirit?

And how prosecute you him who in action is a deceiver and an oppressor,

Yet who also is aggrieved and outraged?

And how shall you punish those whose remorse is already greater than their misdeeds?

Is not remorse the justice which is administered by that very law which you would fain serve?

Yet you cannot lay remorse upon the innocent nor lift it from the heart of the guilty.

Unbidden shall it call in the night, that men may wake and gaze upon themselves.

And you who would understand justice, how shall you unless you look upon all deeds in the fullness of light?

Only then shall you know that the erect and the fallen are but one man standing in twilight between the night of his pigmy-self and the day of his god-self,

And that the corner-stone of the temple is not higher than the lowest stone in its foundation.

Laws

Then a lawyer said, "But what of our Laws, master?"

And he answered:

You delight in laying down laws,

Yet you delight more in breaking them.

Like children playing by the ocean who build sand-towers with constancy and then destroy them with laughter.

But while you build your sand-towers the ocean brings more sand to the shore,

And when you destroy them, the ocean laughs with you.

Verily the ocean laughs always with the innocent.

But what of those to whom life is not an ocean, and man-made laws are not sand-towers,

But to whom life is a rock, and the law a chisel with which they would carve it in their own likeness?

What of the cripple who hates dancers?

What of the ox who loves his yoke and deems the elk and deer of the forest stray and vagrant things?

What of the old serpent who cannot shed his skin, and calls all others naked and shameless?

And of him who comes early to the wedding-feast, and when over-fed and tired goes his way saying that all feasts are violation and all feasters law-breakers?

What shall I say of these save that they too stand in the sunlight, but with their backs to the sun?

They see only their shadows, and their shadows are their laws.

And what is the sun to them but a caster of shadows?

And what is it to acknowledge the laws but to stoop down and trace their shadows upon the earth?

But you who walk facing the sun, what images drawn on the earth can hold you?

You who travel with the wind, what weathervane shall direct your course?

What man's law shall bind you if you break your yoke but upon no man's prison door?

What laws shall you fear if you dance but stumble against no man's iron chains?

And who is he that shall bring you to judgment if you tear off your garment yet leave it in no man's path?

People of Orphalese, you can muffle the drum, and you can loosen the strings of the lyre, but who shall command the skylark not to sing?

Freedom

And an orator said, "Speak to us of Freedom."

And he answered:

At the city gate and by your fireside I have seen you prostrate yourself and worship your own freedom,

Even as slaves humble themselves before a tyrant and praise him though he slays them.

Ay, in the grove of the temple and in the shadow of the citadel I have seen the freest among you wear their freedom as a yoke and a handcuff.

And my heart bled within me; for you can only be free when even the desire of seeking freedom becomes a harness to you, and when you cease to speak of freedom as a goal and a fulfillment.

You shall be free indeed when your days are not without a care nor your nights without a want and a grief,

But rather when these things girdle your life and yet you rise above them naked and unbound.

And how shall you rise beyond your days and nights unless you break the chains which you at the dawn of your understanding have fastened around your noon hour?

In truth that which you call freedom is the strongest of these chains, though its links glitter in the sun and dazzle the eyes.

And what is it but fragments of your own self you would discard that you may become free?

If it is an unjust law you would abolish, that law was written with your own hand upon your own forehead.

You cannot erase it by burning your law books nor by washing the foreheads of your judges, though you pour the sea upon them.

And if it is a despot you would dethrone, see first that his throne erected within you is destroyed.

For how can a tyrant rule the free and the proud, but for a tyranny in their own freedom and a shame in their won pride?

And if it is a care you would cast off, that care has been chosen by you rather than imposed upon you.

And if it is a fear you would dispel, the seat of that fear is in your heart and not in the hand of the feared.

Verily all things move within your being in constant half embrace, the desired and the dreaded, the repugnant and the cherished, the pursued and that which you would escape.

These things move within you as lights and shadows in pairs that cling.

And when the shadow fades and is no more, the light that lingers becomes a shadow to another light.

And thus your freedom when it loses its fetters becomes itself the fetter of a greater freedom.

Reason And Passion

And the priestess spoke again and said: "Speak to us of Reason and Passion."

And he answered saying:

Your soul is oftentimes a battlefield, upon which your reason and your judgment wage war against passion and your appetite.

Would that I could be the peacemaker in your soul, that I might turn the discord and the rivalry of your elements into oneness and melody.

But how shall I, unless you yourselves be also the peacemakers, nay, the lovers of all your elements?

Your reason and your passion are the rudder and the sails of your seafaring soul.

If either your sails or our rudder be broken, you can but toss and drift, or else be held at a standstill in mid-seas.

For reason, ruling alone, is a force confining; and passion, unattended, is a flame that burns to its own destruction.

Therefore let your soul exalt your reason to the height of passion; that it may sing;

And let it direct your passion with reason, that your passion may live through its own daily resurrection, and like the phoenix rise above its own ashes.

I would have you consider your judgment and your appetite even as you would two loved guests in your house.

Surely you would not honor one guest above the other; for he who is more mindful of one loses the love and the faith of both.

Among the hills, when you sit in the cool shade of the white poplars, sharing the peace and serenity of distant fields and meadows - then let your heart say in silence, "God rests in reason."

And when the storm comes, and the mighty wind shakes the forest, and thunder and lightning proclaim the majesty of the sky - then let your heart say in awe, "God moves in passion."

And since you are a breath in God's sphere, and a leaf in God's forest, you too should rest in reason and move in passion.

Pain

And a woman spoke, saying, "Tell us of Pain."

And he said:

Your pain is the breaking of the shell that encloses your understanding.

Even as the stone of the fruit must break, that its heart may stand in the sun, so must you know pain.

And could you keep your heart in wonder at the daily miracles of your life, your pain would not seem less wondrous than your joy;

And you would accept the seasons of your heart, even as you have always accepted the seasons that pass over your fields.

And you would watch with serenity through the winters of your grief.

Much of your pain is self-chosen.

It is the bitter potion by which the physician within you heals your sick self.

Therefore trust the physician, and drink his remedy in silence and tranquility:

For his hand, though heavy and hard, is guided by the tender hand of the Unseen,

And the cup he brings, though it burn your lips, has been fashioned of the clay which the Potter has moistened with His own sacred tears.

Self-Knowledge

And a man said, "Speak to us of Self-Knowledge."

And he answered, saying:

Your hearts know in silence the secrets of the days and the nights.

But your ears thirst for the sound of your heart's knowledge.

You would know in words that which you have always known in thought.

You would touch with your fingers the naked body of your dreams.

And it is well you should.

The hidden well-spring of your soul must needs rise and run murmuring to the sea;

And the treasure of your infinite depths would be revealed to your eyes.

But let there be no scales to weigh your unknown treasure;

And seek not the depths of your knowledge with staff or sounding line.

For self is a sea boundless and measureless.

Say not, "I have found *the* truth," but rather, "I have found *a* truth."

Say not, "I have found the path of the soul." Say rather, "I have met the soul walking upon my path."

For the soul walks upon all paths.

The soul walks not upon a line, neither does it grow like a reed.

The soul unfolds itself, like a lotus of countless petals.

Teaching

Then said a teacher, "Speak to us of Teaching."

And he said:

No man can reveal to you aught but that which already lies half asleep in the dawning of our knowledge.

The teacher who walks in the shadow of the temple, among his followers, gives not of his wisdom but rather of his faith and his lovingness.

If he is indeed wise he does not bid you enter the house of wisdom, but rather leads you to the threshold of your own mind.

The astronomer may speak to you of his understanding of space, but he cannot give you his understanding.

The musician may sing to you of the rhythm which is in all space, but he cannot give you the ear which arrests the rhythm nor the voice that echoes it.

And he who is versed in the science of numbers can tell of the regions of weight and measure, but he cannot conduct you thither.

For the vision of one man lends not its wings to another man.

And even as each one of you stands alone in God's knowledge, so must each one of you be alone in his knowledge of God and in his understanding of the earth.

Friendship

And a youth said, "Speak to us of Friendship."

Your friend is your needs answered.

He is your field which you sow with love and reap with thanksgiving.

And he is your board and your fireside.

For you come to him with your hunger, and you seek him for peace.

When your friend speaks his mind you fear not the "nay" in your own mind, nor do you withhold the "ay."

And when he is silent your heart ceases not to listen to his heart;

For without words, in friendship, all thoughts, all desires, all expectations are born and shared, with joy that is unacclaimed.

When you part from your friend, you grieve not;

For that which you love most in him may be clearer in his absence, as the mountain to the climber is clearer from the plain.

And let there be no purpose in friendship save the deepening of the spirit.

For love that seeks aught but the disclosure of its own mystery is not love but a net cast forth: and only the unprofitable is caught.

And let your best be for your friend.

If he must know the ebb of your tide, let him know its flood also.

For what is your friend that you should seek him with hours to kill?

Seek him always with hours to live.

For it is his to fill your need, but not your emptiness.

And in the sweetness of friendship let there be laughter, and sharing of pleasures.

For in the dew of little things the heart finds its morning and is refreshed.

Talking

And then a scholar said, "Speak of Talking."

And he answered, saying:

You talk when you cease to be at peace with your thoughts;

And when you can no longer dwell in the solitude of your heart you live in your lips, and sound is a diversion and a pastime.

And in much of your talking, thinking is half murdered.

For thought is a bird of space, that in a cage of words many indeed unfold its wings but cannot fly.

There are those among you who seek the talkative through fear of being alone.

The silence of aloneness reveals to their eyes their naked selves and they would escape.

And there are those who talk, and without knowledge or forethought reveal a truth which they themselves do not understand.

And there are those who have the truth within them, but they tell it not in words.

In the bosom of such as these the spirit dwells in rhythmic silence.

When you meet your friend on the roadside or in the market place, let the spirit in you move your lips and direct your tongue.

Let the voice within your voice speak to the ear of his ear;

For his soul will keep the truth of your heart as the taste of the wine is remembered

When the color is forgotten and the vessel is no more.

Time

And an astronomer said, "Master, what of Time?"

And he answered:

You would measure time the measureless and the immeasurable.

You would adjust your conduct and even direct the course of your spirit according to hours and seasons.

Of time you would make a stream upon whose bank you would sit and watch its flowing.

Yet the timeless in you is aware of life's timelessness,

And knows that yesterday is but today's memory and tomorrow is today's dream.

And that that which sings and contemplates in you is still dwelling within the bounds of that first moment which scattered the stars into space.

Who among you does not feel that his power to love is boundless?

And yet who does not feel that very love, though boundless, encompassed within the centre of his being, and moving not form love thought to love thought, nor from love deeds to other love deeds?

And is not time even as love is, undivided and paceless?

But if in you thought you must measure time into seasons, let each season encircle all the other seasons,

And let today embrace the past with remembrance and the future with longing.

Good And Evil

And one of the elders of the city said, "Speak to us of Good and Evil."

And he answered:

Of the good in you I can speak, but not of the evil.

For what is evil but good tortured by its own hunger and thirst?

Verily when good is hungry it seeks food even in dark caves, and when it thirsts, it drinks even of dead waters.

You are good when you are one with yourself.

Yet when you are not one with yourself you are not evil.

For a divided house is not a den of thieves; it is only a divided house.

And a ship without rudder may wander aimlessly among perilous isles yet sink not to the bottom.

You are good when you strive to give of yourself.

Yet you are not evil when you seek gain for yourself.

For when you strive for gain you are but a root that clings to the earth and sucks at her breast.

Surely the fruit cannot say to the root, "Be like me, ripe and full and ever giving of your abundance."

For to the fruit giving is a need, as receiving is a need to the root.

You are good when you are fully awake in your speech,

Yet you are not evil when you sleep while your tongue staggers without purpose.

And even stumbling speech may strengthen a weak tongue.

You are good when you walk to your goal firmly and with bold steps.

Yet you are not evil when you go thither limping.

Even those who limp go not backward.

But you who are strong and swift, see that you do not limp before the lame, deeming it kindness.

You are good in countless ways, and you are not evil when you are not good,

You are only loitering and sluggard.

Pity that the stags cannot teach swiftness to the turtles.

In your longing for your giant self lies your goodness: and that longing is in all of you.

But in some of you that longing is a torrent rushing with might to the sea, carrying the secrets of the hillsides and the songs of the forest.

And in others it is a flat stream that loses itself in angles and bends and lingers before it reaches the shore.

But let not him who longs much say to him who longs little, "Wherefore are you slow and halting?"

For the truly good ask not the naked, "Where is your garment?" nor the houseless, "What has befallen your house?"

Prayer

Then a priestess said, "Speak to us of Prayer."

And he answered, saying:

You pray in your distress and in your need; would that you might pray also in the fullness of your joy and in your days of abundance.

For what is prayer but the expansion of yourself into the living ether?

And if it is for your comfort to pour your darkness into space, it is also for your delight to pour forth the dawning of your heart.

And if you cannot but weep when your soul summons you to prayer, she should spur you again and yet again, though weeping, until you shall come laughing.

When you pray you rise to meet in the air those who are praying at that very hour, and whom save in prayer you may not meet.

Therefore let your visit to that temple invisible be for naught but ecstasy and sweet communion.

For if you should enter the temple for no other purpose than asking you shall not receive.

And if you should enter into it to humble yourself you shall not be lifted:

Or even if you should enter into it to beg for the good of others you shall not be heard.

It is enough that you enter the temple invisible.

I cannot teach you how to pray in words.

God listens not to your words save when He Himself utters them through your lips.

And I cannot teach you the prayer of the seas and the forests and the mountains.

But you who are born of the mountains and the forests and the seas can find their prayer in your heart,

And if you but listen in the stillness of the night you shall hear them saying in silence,

"Our God, who art our winged self, it is thy will in us that willeth.

It is thy desire in us that desireth.

It is thy urge in us that would turn our nights, which are thine, into days which are thine also.

We cannot ask thee for aught, for thou knowest our needs before they are born in us:

Thou art our need; and in giving us more of thyself thou givest us all."

Pleasure

Then a hermit, who visited the city once a year, came forth and said, "Speak to us of Pleasure."

And he answered, saying:

Pleasure is a freedom song,

But it is not freedom.

It is the blossoming of your desires,

But it is not their fruit.

It is a depth calling unto a height,

But it is not the deep nor the high.

It is the caged taking wing,

But it is not space encompassed.

Ay, in very truth, pleasure is a freedom-song.

And I fain would have you sing it with fullness of heart; yet I would not have you lose your hearts in the singing.

Some of your youth seek pleasure as if it were all, and they are judged and rebuked.

I would not judge nor rebuke them. I would have them seek.

For they shall find pleasure, but not her alone:

Seven are her sisters, and the least of them is more beautiful than pleasure.

Have you not heard of the man who was digging in the earth for roots and found a treasure?

And some of your elders remember pleasures with regret like wrongs committed in drunkenness.

But regret is the beclouding of the mind and not its chastisement.

They should remember their pleasures with gratitude, as they would the harvest of a summer.

Yet if it comforts them to regret, let them be comforted.

And there are among you those who are neither young to seek nor old to remember;

And in their fear of seeking and remembering they shun all pleasures, lest they neglect the spirit or offend against it.

But even in their foregoing is their pleasure.

And thus they too find a treasure though they dig for roots with quivering hands.

But tell me, who is he that can offend the spirit?

Shall the nightingale offend the stillness of the night, or the firefly the stars?

And shall your flame or your smoke burden the wind?

Think you the spirit is a still pool which you can trouble with a staff?

Oftentimes in denying yourself pleasure you do but store the desire in the recesses of your being.

Who knows but that which seems omitted today, waits for tomorrow?

Even your body knows its heritage and its rightful need and will not be deceived.

And your body is the harp of your soul,

And it is yours to bring forth sweet music from it or confused sounds.

And now you ask in your heart, "How shall we distinguish that which is good in pleasure from that which is not good?"

Go to your fields and your gardens, and you shall learn that it is the pleasure of the bee to gather honey of the flower,

But it is also the pleasure of the flower to yield its honey to the bee.

For to the bee a flower is a fountain of life,

And to the flower a bee is a messenger of love,

And to both, bee and flower, the giving and the receiving of pleasure is a need and an ecstasy.

People of Orphalese, be in your pleasures like the flowers and the bees.

Beauty

And a poet said, "Speak to us of Beauty."

Where shall you seek beauty, and how shall you find her unless she herself be your way and your guide?

And how shall you speak of her except she be the weaver of your speech?

The aggrieved and the injured say, "Beauty is kind and gentle.

Like a young mother half-shy of her own glory she walks among us."

And the passionate say, "Nay, beauty is a thing of might and dread.

Like the tempest she shakes the earth beneath us and the sky above us."

The tired and the weary say, "Beauty is of soft whisperings. She speaks in our spirit.

Her voice yields to our silences like a faint light that quivers in fear of the shadow."

But the restless say, "We have heard her shouting among the mountains,

And with her cries came the sound of hoofs, and the beating of wings and the roaring of lions."

At night the watchmen of the city say, "Beauty shall rise with the dawn from the east."

And at noontide the toilers and the wayfarers say, "We have seen her leaning over the earth from the windows of the sunset."

In winter say the snow-bound, "She shall come with the spring leaping upon the hills."

And in the summer heat the reapers say, "We have seen her dancing with the autumn leaves, and we saw a drift of snow in her hair."

All these things have you said of beauty.

Yet in truth you spoke not of her but of needs unsatisfied,

And beauty is not a need but an ecstasy.

It is not a mouth thirsting nor an empty hand stretched forth,

But rather a heart enflamed and a soul enchanted.

It is not the image you would see nor the song you would hear,

But rather an image you see though you close your eyes and a song you hear though you shut your ears.

It is not the sap within the furrowed bark, nor a wing attached to a claw,

But rather a garden forever in bloom and a flock of angels for ever in flight.

People of Orphalese, beauty is life when life unveils her holy face.

But you are life and you are the veil.

Beauty is eternity gazing at itself in a mirror.
But you are eternity and you are the mirror.

Religion

And an old priest said, "Speak to us of Religion."
And he said:
Have I spoken this day of aught else?
Is not religion all deeds and all reflection,
And that which is neither deed nor reflection, but a wonder and a surprise ever springing in the soul, even while the hands hew the stone or tend the loom?
Who can separate his faith from his actions, or his belief from his occupations?
Who can spread his hours before him, saying, "This for God and this for myself; This for my soul, and this other for my body?"
All your hours are wings that beat through space from self to self.
He who wears his morality but as his best garment were better naked.
The wind and the sun will tear no holes in his skin.
And he who defines his conduct by ethics imprisons his song-bird in a cage.
The freest song comes not through bars and wires.
And he to whom worshipping is a window, to open but also to shut, has not yet visited the house of his soul whose windows are from dawn to dawn.
Your daily life is your temple and your religion.
Whenever you enter into it take with you your all.
Take the plough and the forge and the mallet and the lute,
The things you have fashioned in necessity or for delight.

For in reverie you cannot rise above your achievements nor fall lower than your failures.

And take with you all men:

For in adoration you cannot fly higher than their hopes nor humble yourself lower than their despair.

And if you would know God be not therefore a solver of riddles.

Rather look about you and you shall see Him playing with your children.

And look into space; you shall see Him walking in the cloud, outstretching His arms in the lightning and descending in rain.

You shall see Him smiling in flowers, then rising and waving His hands in trees.

Death

Than Almitra spoke, saying, "We would ask now of Death."

And he said:

You would know the secret of death.

But how shall you find it unless you seek it in the heart of life?

The owl whose night-bound eyes are blind unto the day cannot unveil the mystery of light.

If you would indeed behold the spirit of death, open your heart wide unto the body of life.

For life and death are one, even as the river and the sea are one.

In the depth of your hopes and desires lies your silent knowledge of the beyond;

And like seeds dreaming beneath the snow your heart dreams of spring.

Trust the dreams, for in them is hidden the gate to eternity.

Your fear of death is but the trembling of the shepherd when he stands before the king whose hand is to be laid upon him in honor.

Is the sheered not joyful beneath his trembling, that he shall wear the mark of the king?

Yet is he not more mindful of his trembling?

For what is it to die but to stand naked in the wind and to melt into the sun?

And what is to cease breathing, but to free the breath from its restless tides, that it may rise and expand and seek God unencumbered?

Only when you drink from the river of silence shall you indeed sing.

And when you have reached the mountain top, then you shall begin to climb.

And when the earth shall claim your limbs, then shall you truly dance.

The Farewell

And now it was evening.

And Almitra the seeress said, "Blessed be this day and this place and your spirit that has spoken."

And he answered, Was it I who spoke? Was I not also a listener?

Then he descended the steps of the Temple and all the people followed him. And he reached his ship and stood upon the deck.

And facing the people again, he raised his voice and said:

People of Orphalese, the wind bids me leave you.

Less hasty am I than the wind, yet I must go.

We wanderers, ever seeking the lonelier way, begin no day where we have ended another day; and no sunrise finds us where sunset left us.

Even while the earth sleeps we travel.

We are the seeds of the tenacious plant, and it is in our ripeness and our fullness of heart that we are given to the wind and are scattered.

Brief were my days among you, and briefer still the words I have spoken.

But should my voice fade in your ears, and my love vanish in your memory, then I will come again,

And with a richer heart and lips more yielding to the spirit will I speak.

Yea, I shall return with the tide,

And though death may hide me, and the greater silence enfold me, yet again will I seek your understanding.

And not in vain will I seek.

If aught I have said is truth, that truth shall reveal itself in a clearer voice, and in words more kin to your thoughts.

I go with the wind, people of Orphalese, but not down into emptiness;

And if this day is not a fulfillment of your needs and my love, then let it be a promise till another day. Know therefore, that from the greater silence I shall return.

The mist that drifts away at dawn, leaving but dew in the fields, shall rise and gather into a cloud and then fall down in rain.

And not unlike the mist have I been.

In the stillness of the night I have walked in your streets, and my spirit has entered your houses,

And your heart-beats were in my heart, and your breath was upon my face, and I knew you all.

Ay, I knew your joy and your pain, and in your sleep your dreams were my dreams.

And oftentimes I was among you a lake among the mountains.

I mirrored the summits in you and the bending slopes, and even the passing flocks of your thoughts and your desires.

And to my silence came the laughter of your children in streams, and the longing of your youths in rivers.

And when they reached my depth the streams and the rivers ceased not yet to sing.

But sweeter still than laughter and greater than longing came to me.

It was boundless in you;

The vast man in whom you are all but cells and sinews;

He in whose chant all your singing is but a soundless throbbing.

It is in the vast man that you are vast,

And in beholding him that I beheld you and loved you.

For what distances can love reach that are not in that vast sphere?

What visions, what expectations and what presumptions can outsoar that flight?

Like a giant oak tree covered with apple blossoms is the vast man in you.

His mind binds you to the earth, his fragrance lifts you into space, and in his durability you are deathless.

You have been told that, even like a chain, you are as weak as your weakest link.

This is but half the truth. You are also as strong as your strongest link.

To measure you by your smallest deed is to reckon the power of ocean by the frailty of its foam.

To judge you by your failures is to cast blame upon the seasons for their inconsistency.

Ay, you are like an ocean,

And though heavy-grounded ships await the tide upon your shores, yet, even like an ocean, you cannot hasten your tides.

And like the seasons you are also,

And though in your winter you deny your spring,

Yet spring, reposing within you, smiles in her drowsiness and is not offended.

Think not I say these things in order that you may say the one to the other, "He praised us well. He saw but the good in us."

I only speak to you in words of that which you yourselves know in thought.

And what is word knowledge but a shadow of wordless knowledge?

Your thoughts and my words are waves from a sealed memory that keeps records of our yesterdays,

And of the ancient days when the earth knew not us nor herself,

And of nights when earth was upwrought with confusion,

Wise men have come to you to give you of their wisdom. I came to take of your wisdom:

And behold I have found that which is greater than wisdom.

It is a flame spirit in you ever gathering more of itself,

While you, heedless of its expansion, bewail the withering of your days.

It is life in quest of life in bodies that fear the grave.

There are no graves here.

These mountains and plains are a cradle and a stepping-stone.

Whenever you pass by the field where you have laid your ancestors look well thereupon, and you shall see yourselves and your children dancing hand in hand.

Verily you often make merry without knowing.

Others have come to you to whom for golden promises made unto your faith you have given but riches and power and glory.

Less than a promise have I given, and yet more generous have you been to me.

You have given me deeper thirsting after life.

Surely there is no greater gift to a man than that which turns all his aims into parching lips and all life into a fountain.

And in this lies my honor and my reward -

That whenever I come to the fountain to drink I find the living water itself thirsty;

And it drinks me while I drink it.

Some of you have deemed me proud and over-shy to receive gifts.

To proud indeed am I to receive wages, but not gifts.

And though I have eaten berries among the hill when you would have had me sit at your board,

And slept in the portico of the temple where you would gladly have sheltered me,

Yet was it not your loving mindfulness of my days and my nights that made food sweet to my mouth and girdled my sleep with visions?

For this I bless you most:

You give much and know not that you give at all.

Verily the kindness that gazes upon itself in a mirror turns to stone,

And a good deed that calls itself by tender names becomes the parent to a curse.

And some of you have called me aloof, and drunk with my own aloneness,

And you have said, "He holds council with the trees of the forest, but not with men.

He sits alone on hill-tops and looks down upon our city."

True it is that I have climbed the hills and walked in remote places.

How could I have seen you save from a great height or a great distance?

How can one be indeed near unless he be far?

And others among you called unto me, not in words, and they said,

"Stranger, stranger, lover of unreachable heights, why dwell you among the summits where eagles build their nests?

Why seek you the unattainable?

What storms would you trap in your net,

And what vaporous birds do you hunt in the sky?

Come and be one of us.

Descend and appease your hunger with our bread and quench your thirst with our wine."

In the solitude of their souls they said these things;

But were their solitude deeper they would have known that I sought but the secret of your joy and your pain,

And I hunted only your larger selves that walk the sky.

But the hunter was also the hunted:

For many of my arrows left my bow only to seek my own breast.

And the flier was also the creeper;

For when my wings were spread in the sun their shadow upon the earth was a turtle.

And I the believer was also the doubter;

For often have I put my finger in my own wound that I might have the greater belief in you and the greater knowledge of you.

And it is with this belief and this knowledge that I say,

You are not enclosed within your bodies, nor confined to houses or fields.

That which is you dwells above the mountain and roves with the wind.

It is not a thing that crawls into the sun for warmth or digs holes into darkness for safety,

But a thing free, a spirit that envelops the earth and moves in the ether.

If this be vague words, then seek not to clear them.

Vague and nebulous is the beginning of all things, but not their end,

And I fain would have you remember me as a beginning.

Life, and all that lives, is conceived in the mist and not in the crystal.

And who knows but a crystal is mist in decay?

This would I have you remember in remembering me:

That which seems most feeble and bewildered in you is the strongest and most determined.

Is it not your breath that has erected and hardened the structure of your bones?

And is it not a dream which none of you remember having dreamt that building your city and fashioned all there is in it?

Could you but see the tides of that breath you would cease to see all else,

And if you could hear the whispering of the dream you would hear no other sound.

But you do not see, nor do you hear, and it is well.

The veil that clouds your eyes shall be lifted by the hands that wove it,

And the clay that fills your ears shall be pierced by those fingers that kneaded it.

And you shall see

And you shall hear.

Yet you shall not deplore having known blindness, nor regret having been deaf.

For in that day you shall know the hidden purposes in all things,

And you shall bless darkness as you would bless light.

After saying these things he looked about him, and he saw the pilot of his ship standing by the helm and gazing now at the full sails and now at the distance.

And he said:

Patient, over-patient, is the captain of my ship.

The wind blows, and restless are the sails;

Even the rudder begs direction;

Yet quietly my captain awaits my silence.

And these my mariners, who have heard the choir of the greater sea, they too have heard me patiently.

Now they shall wait no longer.

I am ready.

The stream has reached the sea, and once more the great mother holds her son against her breast.

Fare you well, people of Orphalese.

This day has ended.

It is closing upon us even as the water-lily upon its own tomorrow.

What was given us here we shall keep,

And if it suffices not, then again must we come together and together stretch our hands unto the giver.

Forget not that I shall come back to you.

A little while, and my longing shall gather dust and foam for another body.

A little while, a moment of rest upon the wind, and another woman shall bear me.

Farewell to you and the youth I have spent with you.

It was but yesterday we met in a dream.

You have sung to me in my aloneness, and I of your longings have built a tower in the sky.

But now our sleep has fled and our dream is over, and it is no longer dawn.

The noontide is upon us and our half waking has turned to fuller day, and we must part.

If in the twilight of memory we should meet once more, we shall speak again together and you shall sing to me a deeper song.

And if our hands should meet in another dream, we shall build another tower in the sky.

So saying he made a signal to the seamen, and straightaway they weighed anchor and cast the ship loose from its moorings, and they moved eastward.

And a cry came from the people as from a single heart, and it rose the dusk and was carried out over the sea like a great trumpeting.

Only Almitra was silent, gazing after the ship until it had vanished into the mist.

And when all the people were dispersed she still stood alone upon the sea-wall, remembering in her heart his saying,

A little while, a moment of rest upon the wind, and another woman shall bear me."

The Madman
His Parables And Poems
1918

How I Became A Madman

You ask me how I became a madman. It happened thus: One day, long before many gods were born, I woke from a deep sleep and found all my masks were stolen — the seven masks I have fashioned and worn in seven lives — I ran maskless through the crowded streets shouting, "Thieves, thieves, the cursed thieves."

Men and women laughed at me and some ran to their houses in fear of me.

And when I reached the market place, a youth standing on a house-top cried, "He is a madman." I looked up to behold him; the sun kissed my own naked face for the first time. For the first time the sun kissed my own naked face and my soul was inflamed with love for the sun, and I wanted my masks no more. And as if in a trance I cried, "Blessed, blessed are the thieves who stole my masks."

Thus I became a madman.

And I have found both freedom and safety in my madness; the freedom of loneliness and the safety from being understood, for those who understand us enslave something in us.

But let me not be too proud of my safety. Even a Thief in a jail is safe from another thief.

God

In the ancient days, when the first quiver of speech came to my lips, I ascended the holy mountain and spoke unto God, saying, "Master, I am thy slave. Thy hidden will is my law and I shall obey thee for ever more."

But God made no answer, and like a mighty tempest passed away.

And after a thousand years I ascended the holy mountain and again spoke unto God, saying, "Creator, I am thy creation. Out of clay hast thou fashioned me and to thee I owe mine all."

And God made no answer, but like a thousand swift wings passed away.

And after a thousand years I climbed the holy mountain and spoke unto God again, saying, "Father, I am thy son. In pity and love thou hast given me birth, and through love and worship I shall inherit thy kingdom."

And God made no answer, and like the mist that veils the distant hills he passed away.

And after a thousand years I climbed the sacred mountain and again spoke unto God, saying, "My God, my aim and my fulfilment; I am thy yesterday and thou art my tomorrow. I am thy root in the earth and thou art my flower in the sky, and together we grow before the face of the sun."

Then God leaned over me, and in my ears whispered words of sweetness, and even as the sea that enfoldeth a brook that runneth down to her, he enfolded me.

And when I descended to the valleys and the plains God was there also.

My Friend

My friend, I am not what I seem. Seeming is but a garment I wear—a care-woven garment that protects me from thy questionings and thee from my negligence.

The "I" in me, my friend, dwells in the house of silence, and therein it shall remain for ever more, unperceived, unapproachable.

I would not have thee believe in what I say nor trust in what I do—for my words are naught but thy own thoughts in sound and my deeds thy own hopes in action.

When thou sayest, "The wind bloweth eastward," I say, "Aye, it doth blow eastward"; for I would not have thee know that my mind doth not dwell upon the wind but upon the sea.

Thou canst not understand my seafaring thoughts, nor would I have thee understand. I would be at sea alone.

When it is day with thee, my friend, it is night with me; yet even then I speak of the noontide that dances upon the hills and of the purple shadow that steals its way across the valley; for thou canst not hear the songs of my darkness nor see my wings beating against the stars—and I fain would not have thee hear or see. I would be with night alone.

When thou ascendest to thy Heaven I descend to my Hell—even then thou callest to me across the unbridgeable gulf, "My companion, my comrade," and I call back to thee, "My comrade, my companion"—for I would not have thee see my Hell. The flame would burn thy eyesight and the smoke would crowd thy nostrils. And I love my Hell too well to have thee visit it. I would be in Hell alone.

Thou lovest Truth and Beauty and Righteousness; and I for thy sake say it is well and seemly to love these things. But in my heart I laugh at thy love. Yet I would not have thee see my laughter. I would laugh alone.

My friend, thou art good and cautious and wise; nay, thou art perfect—and I, too, speak with thee wisely and cautiously. And yet I am mad. But I mask my madness. I would be mad alone.

My friend, thou art not my friend, but how shall I make thee understand? My path is not thy path, yet together we walk, hand in hand.

The Scarecrow

Once I said to a scarecrow, "You must be tired of standing in this lonely field."

And he said, "The joy of scaring is a deep and lasting one, and I never tire of it."

Said I, after a minute of thought, "It is true; for I too have known that joy."

Said he, "Only those who are stuffed with straw can know it."

Then I left him, not knowing whether he had complimented or belittled me.

A year passed, during which the scarecrow turned philosopher.

And when I passed by him again I saw two crows building a nest under his hat.

The Sleep-Walkers

In the town where I was born lived a woman and her daughter, who walked in their sleep.

One night, while silence enfolded the world, the woman and her daughter, walking, yet asleep, met in their mist-veiled garden.

And the mother spoke, and she said: "At last, at last, my enemy! You by whom my youth was destroyed — who have built up your life upon the ruins of mine! Would I could kill you!"

And the daughter spoke, and she said: "O hateful woman, selfish and old! Who stand between my freer self and me! Who would have my life an echo of your own faded life! Would you were dead!"

At that moment a cock crew, and both women awoke. The mother said gently, "Is that you, darling?" And the daughter answered gently, "Yes, dear."

The Wise Dog

One day there passed by a company of cats a wise dog.

And as he came near and saw that they were very intent and heeded him not, he stopped.

Then there arose in the midst of the company a large, grave cat and looked upon them and said, "Brethren, pray ye; and when ye have prayed again and yet again, nothing doubting, verily then it shall rain mice."

And when the dog heard this he laughed in his heart and turned from them saying, "O blind and foolish cats, has it not been written and have I not known and my fathers before me, that that which raineth for prayer and faith and supplication is not mice but bones."

The Two Hermits

Upon a lonely mountain, there lived two hermits who worshipped God and loved one another.

Now these two hermits had one earthen bowl, and this was their only possession.

One day an evil spirit entered into the heart of the older hermit and he came to the younger and said, "It is long that we have lived together. The time has come for us to part. Let us divide our possessions."

Then the younger hermit was saddened and he said, "It grieves me, Brother, that thou shouldst leave me. But if thou must needs go, so be it," and he brought the earthen bowl and gave it to him saying, "We cannot divide it, Brother, let it be thine."

Then the older hermit said, "Charity I will not accept. I will take nothing but mine own. It must be divided."

And the younger one said, "If the bowl be broken, of what use would it be to thee or to me? If it be thy pleasure let us rather cast a lot."

On Giving and Taking

Once there lived a man who had a valley full of needles.

And one day the mother of Jesus came to him and said: "Friend, my son's garment is torn and I must needs mend it before he goeth to the temple. Wouldst thou not give me a needle?"

And he gave her not a needle, but he gave her a learned discourse on Giving and Taking to carry to her son before he should go to the temple.

The Seven Selves

In the silent hour of the night, as I lay half asleep, my seven selves sat together and thus conversed in whispers:

First Self: Here, in this madman, I have dwelt all these years, with naught to do but renew his pain by day and recreate his sorrow by night. I can bear my fate no longer, and now I must rebel.

Second Self: Yours is a better lot than mine, brother, for it is given me to be this madman's joyous self. I laugh his laughter and sing his happy hours, and with thrice winged feet I dance his brighter thoughts. It is I that would rebel against my weary existence.

Third Self: And what of me, the love-ridden self, the flaming brand of wild passion and fantastic desires? It is I the love-sick self who would rebel against this madman.

Fourth Self: I, amongst you all, am the most miserable, for naught was given me but the odious hatred and destructive loathing. It is I, the tempest-like self, the one born in the black caves of Hell, who would protest against serving this madman.

Fifth Self: Nay, it is I, the thinking self, the fanciful self, the self of hunger and thirst, the one doomed to wander without rest in search of unknown things and things not yet created; it is I, not you, who would rebel.

Sixth Self: And I, the working self, the pitiful laborer, who, with patient hands, and longing eyes, fashion the days into images and give the formless elements new and eternal forms—it is I, the solitary one, who would rebel against this restless madman.

Seventh Self: How strange that you all would rebel against this man, because each and every one of you has a preordained fate to fulfil. Ah! could I but be like one of you, a self with a determined lot! But I have none, I am the do-nothing self, the one who sits in the dumb, empty nowhere and nowhen, when you are busy re-creating life. Is it you or I, neighbors, who should rebel?

When the seventh self thus spake the other six selves looked with pity upon him but said nothing more; and as the night grew deeper one after the other went to sleep enfolded with a new and happy submission.

But the seventh self remained watching and gazing at nothingness, which is behind all things.

War

One night a feast was held in the palace, and there came a man and prostrated himself before the prince, and all the feasters looked upon him; and they saw that one of his eyes was out and that the empty socket bled. And the prince inquired of him, "What has befallen you?" And the man replied, "O prince, I am by profession a thief, and this night, because there was no moon, I went to rob the money-changer's shop, and as I climbed in through the window I made a mistake and entered the weaver's shop, and in the dark I ran into the weaver's loom and my eye was plucked out. And now, O prince, I ask for justice upon the weaver."

Then the prince sent for the weaver and he came, and it was decreed that one of his eyes should be plucked out.

"O prince," said the weaver, "the decree is just. It is right that one of my eyes be taken. And yet, alas! both are necessary to me in order that I may see the two sides of the cloth that I weave. But I have a neighbor, a cobbler, who has also two eyes, and in his trade both eyes are not necessary."

Then the prince sent for the cobbler. And he came. And they took out one of the cobbler's two eyes.

And justice was satisfied.

The Fox

A fox looked at his shadow at sunrise and said, "I will have a camel for lunch today." And all morning he went about looking for camels. But at noon he saw his shadow again—and he said, "A mouse will do."

The Wise King

Once there ruled in the distant city of Wirani a king who was both mighty and wise. And he was feared for his might and loved for his wisdom.

Now, in the heart of that city was a well, whose water was cool and crystalline, from which all the inhabitants drank, even the king and his courtiers; for there was no other well.

One night when all were asleep, a witch entered the city, and poured seven drops of strange liquid into the well, and said, "From this hour he who drinks this water shall become mad."

Next morning all the inhabitants, save the king and his lord chamberlain, drank from the well and became mad, even as the witch had foretold.

And during that day the people in the narrow streets and in the market places did naught but whisper to one another, "The king is mad. Our king and his lord chamberlain have lost their reason. Surely we cannot be ruled by a mad king. We must dethrone him."

That evening the king ordered a golden goblet to be filled from the well. And when it was brought to him he drank deeply, and gave it to his lord chamberlain to drink.

And there was great rejoicing in that distant city of Wirani, because its king and its lord chamberlain had regained their reason.

Ambition

Three men met at a tavern table. One was a weaver, another a carpenter and the third a ploughman.

Said the weaver, "I sold a fine linen shroud today for two pieces of gold. Let us have all the wine we went."

"And I," said the carpenter, "I sold my best coffin. We will have a great roast with the wine."

"I only dug a grave," said the ploughman, "but my patron paid me double. Let us have honey cakes too."

And all that evening the tavern was busy, for they called often for wine and meat and cakes. And they were merry.

And the host rubbed his hands and smiled at his wife; for his guests were spending freely.

When they left the moon was high, and they walked along the road singing and shouting together.

The host and his wife stood in the tavern door and looked after them.

"Ah!" said the wife, "these gentlemen! So freehanded and so gay! If only they could bring us such luck every day! Then our son need not be a tavern-keeper and work hard. We could educate him, and he could become a priest."

The New Pleasure

Last night I invented a new pleasure, and as I was giving it the first trial an angel and a devil came rushing toward my house. They met at my door and fought with each other over my newly created pleasure; the one crying, "It is a sin!"—the other, "It is a virtue!"

The Other Language

Three days after I was born, as I lay in my silken cradle, gazing with astonished dismay on the new world round about me, my mother spoke to the wet-nurse, saying, "How is my child?"

And the wet-nurse answered, "He does well madame, I have fed him three times; and never before have I seen a babe so young yet so gay."

And I was indignant; and I cried, "It is not true, mother; for my bed is hard, and the milk I have sucked is bitter to my mouth, and the odour of the breast is foul in my nostrils, and I am most miserable."

But my mother did not understand, nor did the nurse; for the language I spoke was that of the world from which I came.

And on the twenty-first day of my life, as I was being christened, the priest said to my mother, "You should indeed be happy, madame, that your son was born a Christian."

And I was surprised, and I said to the priest, "Then your mother in Heaven should be unhappy, for you were not born a Christian."

But the priest too did not understand my language.

And after seven moons, one day a soothsayer looked at me, and he said to my mother, "Your son will be a statesman and a great leader of men."

But I cried out, "That is a false prophecy; for I shall be a musician, and naught but a musician shall I be."

But even at that age my language was not understood—and great was my astonishment.

And after three and thirty years, during which my mother, and the nurse, and the priest have all died, (the shadow of God be upon their spirits) the soothsayer still lives. And yesterday I met him near the gate of the temple; and while we were talking together he said, "I have always known you would become a great musician. Even in your infancy I prophesied and foretold your future."

And I believed him—for now I too have forgotten the language of that other world.

The Pomegranate

Once when I was living in the heart of a pomegranate, I heard a seed saying, "Someday I shall become a tree, and the wind will sing in my branches, and the sun will dance on my leaves, and I shall be strong and beautiful through all the seasons."

Then another seed spoke and said, "When I was as young as you, I too held such views; but now that I can weigh and measure things, I see that my hopes were vain."

And a third seed spoke also, "I see in us nothing that promises so great a future."

And a fourth said, "But what a mockery our life would be, without a greater future!"

Said a fifth, "Why dispute what we shall be, when we know not even what we are."

But a sixth replied, "Whatever we are, that we shall continue to be."

And a seventh said, "I have such a clear idea how everything will be, but I cannot put it into words."

Then an eighth spoke, and a ninth—and a tenth—and then many—until all were speaking, and I could distinguish nothing for the many voices.

And so I moved that very day into the heart of a quince, where the seeds are few and almost silent.

The Two Cages

In my father's garden there are two cages. In one is a lion, which my father's slaves brought from the desert of Ninavah; in the other is a songless sparrow.

Every day at dawn the sparrow calls to the lion, "Good morrow to thee, brother prisoner."

The Three Ants

Three ants met on the nose of a man who was lying asleep in the sun. And after they had saluted one another, each according to the custom of his tribe, they stood there conversing.

The first and said, "These hills and plains are the most barren I have known. I have searched all day for a grain of some sort, and there is none to be found."

Said the second ant, "I too have found nothing, though I have visited every nook and glade. This is, I believe, what my people call the soft, moving land where nothing grows."

Then the third ant raised his head and said, "My friends, we are standing now on the nose of the Supreme Ant, the mighty and infinite Ant, whose body is so great that we cannot see it, whose shadow is so vast that we cannot trace it, whose voice is so loud that we cannot hear it; and He is omnipresent."

When the third ant spoke thus the other ants looked at each other and laughed.

At that moment the man moved and in his sleep raised his hand and scratched his nose, and the three ants were crushed.

The Grave-Digger

Once, as I was burying one of my dead selves, the grave-digger came by and said to me, "Of all those who come here to bury, you alone I like."

Said I, "You please me exceedingly, but why do you like me?"

"Because," said he, "They come weeping and go weeping — you only come laughing and go laughing."

On The Steps Of The Temple

Yestereve, on the marble steps of the Temple, I saw a woman sitting between two men. One side of her face was pale, the other was blushing.

The Blessed City

In my youth I was told that in a certain city every one lived according to the Scriptures.

And I said, "I will seek that city and the blessedness thereof." And it was far. And I made great provision for my journey. And after forty-days I beheld the city and on the forty-first day I entered into it.

And lo! the whole company of the inhabitants had each but a single eye and but one hand. And I was astonished and said to myself, "Shall they of this so holy city have but one eye and one hand?"

Then I saw that they too were astonished, for they were marveling greatly at my two hands and my two eyes. And as they were speaking together I inquired of them saying, "Is this indeed the Blessed City, where each man lives according to the Scriptures?" And they said, "Yes, this is that city."

"And what," said I, "hath befallen you, and where are your right eyes and your right hands?"

And all the people were moved. And they said, "Come thou and see."

And they took me to the temple in the midst of the city. And in the temple I saw a heap of hands and eyes. All withered. Then said I, "Alas! what conqueror hath committed this cruelty upon you?"

And there went a murmur amongst them. And one of their elders stood forth and said, "This doing is of ourselves. God hath made us conquerors over the evil that was in us."

And he led me to a high altar, and all the people followed. And he showed me above the altar an inscription graven, and I read:

"If thy right eye offend thee, pluck it out and cast it from thee; for it is profitable for thee that one of thy members should perish, and not that thy whole body should be cast into hell. And if thy right hand offend thee, cut if off and cast it from thee; for it is profitable for thee that one of thy members should perish, and not that thy whole body should be cast into hell."

Then I understood. And I turned about to all the people and cried, "Hath no man or woman among you two eyes or two hands?"

And they answered me saying, "No, not one. There is none whole save such as are yet too young to read the Scripture and to understand its commandment."

And when we had come out of the temple, I straightway left that Blessed City; for I was not too young, and I could read the scripture.

The Good God And The Evil God

The Good God and the Evil God met on the mountain top.

The Good God said, "Good day to you, brother."

The Evil God made no answer.

And the Good God said, "You are in a bad humour today."

"Yes," said the Evil God, "for of late I have been often mistaken for you, called by your name, and treated as if I were you, and it ill-pleases me."

And the Good God said. "But I too have been mistaken for you and called by your name."

The Evil God walked away cursing the stupidity of man.

"Defeat"

Defeat, my Defeat, my solitude and my aloofness;
You are dearer to me than a thousand triumphs,
And sweeter to my heart than all world glory.

Defeat, my Defeat, my self-knowledge and my defiance,

Through you I know that I am yet young and swift of foot

And not to be trapped by withering laurels.

And in you I have found aloneness

And the joy of being shunned and scorned.

Defeat, my Defeat, my shining sword and shield,

In your eyes I have read

That to be enthroned is to be enslaved,

And to be understood is to be levelled down,

And to be grasped is but to reach one's fullness

And like a ripe fruit to fall and be consumed.

Defeat, my Defeat, my bold companion,

You shall hear my songs and my cries and my silences,

And none but you shall speak to me of the beating of wings,

And urging of seas,

And of mountains that burn in the night,

And you alone shall climb my steep and rocky soul.

Defeat, my Defeat, my deathless courage,

You and I shall laugh together with the storm,

And together we shall dig graves for all that die in us,

And we shall stand in the sun with a will,

And we shall be dangerous.

Night And The Madman

"I am like thee, O, Night, dark and naked; I walk on the flaming path which is above my day-dreams, and whenever my foot touches earth a giant oak tree comes forth."

"Nay, thou art not like me, O, Madman, for thou still lookest backward to see how large a foot-print thou leavest on the sand."

"I am like thee, O, Night, silent and deep; and in the heart of my loneliness lies a Goddess in child-bed; and in him who is being born Heaven touches Hell."

"Nay, thou art not like me, O, Madman, for thou shudderest yet before pain, and the song of the abyss terrifies thee."

"I am like thee, O, Night, wild and terrible; for my ears are crowded with cries of conquered nations and sighs for forgotten lands."

"Nay, thou art not like me, O, Madman, for thou still takest thy little-self for a comrade, and with thy monster-self thou canst not be friend."

"I am like thee, O, Night, cruel and awful; for my bosom is lit by burning ships at sea, and my lips are wet with blood of slain warriors."

"Nay, thou art not like me, O, Madman; for the desire for a sister-spirit is yet upon thee, and thou hast not become a law unto thyself."

"I am like thee, O, Night, joyous and glad; for he who dwells in my shadow is now drunk with virgin wine, and she who follows me is sinning mirthfully."

"Nay, thou art not like me, O, Madman, for thy soul is wrapped in the veil of seven folds and thou holdest not thy heart in thine hand."

"I am like thee, O, Night, patient and passionate; for in my breast a thousand dead lovers are buried in shrouds of withered kisses."

"Yea, Madman, art thou like me? Art thou like me? And canst thou ride the tempest as a steed, and grasp the lightning as a sword?"

"Like thee, O, Night, like thee, mighty and high, and my throne is built upon heaps of fallen Gods; and before me too pass the days to kiss the hem of my garment but never to gaze at my face."

"Art thou like me, child of my darkest heart? And dost thou think my untamed thoughts and speak my vast language?"

"Yea, we are twin brothers, O, Night; for thou revealest space and I reveal my soul."

Faces

I have seen a face with a thousand countenances, and a face that was but a single countenance as if held in a mould.

I have seen a face whose sheen I could look through to the ugliness beneath, and a face whose sheen I had to lift to see how beautiful it was.

I have seen an old face much lined with nothing, and a smooth face in which all things were graven.

I know faces, because I look through the fabric my own eye weaves, and behold the reality beneath.

The Greater Sea

My soul and I went down to the great sea to bathe. And when we reached the shore, we went about looking for a hidden and lonely place.

But as we walked, we saw a man sitting on a grey rock taking pinches of salt from a bag and throwing them into the sea.

"This is the pessimist," said my soul, "Let us leave this place. We cannot bathe here."

We walked on until we reached an inlet. There we saw, standing on a white rock, a man holding a bejeweled box, from which he took sugar and threw it into the sea.

"And this is the optimist," said my soul, "And he too must not see our naked bodies."

Further on we walked. And on a beach we saw a man picking up dead fish and tenderly putting them back into the water.

"And we cannot bathe before him," said my soul. "He is the humane philanthropist."

And we passed on.

Then we came where we saw a man tracing his shadow on the sand. Great waves came and erased it. But he went on tracing it again and again.

"He is the mystic," said my soul, "Let us leave him."

And we walked on, till in a quiet cove we saw a man scooping up the foam and putting it into an alabaster bowl.

"He is the idealist," said my soul, "Surely he must not see our nudity."

And on we walked. Suddenly we heard a voice crying, "This is the sea. This is the deep sea. This is the vast and mighty sea." And when we reached the voice it was a man whose back was turned to the sea, and at his ear he held a shell, listening to its murmur.

And my soul said, "Let us pass on. He is the realist, who turns his back on the whole he cannot grasp, and busies himself with a fragment."

So we passed on. And in a weedy place among the rocks was a man with his head buried in the sand. And I said to my soul, "We can bathe here, for he cannot see us."

"Nay," said my soul, "For he is the most deadly of them all. He is the puritan."

Then a great sadness came over the face of my soul, and into her voice.

"Let us go hence," she said, "For there is no lonely, hidden place where we can bathe. I would not have this wind lift my golden hair, or bare my white bosom in this air, or let the light disclose my scared nakedness."

Then we left that sea to seek the Greater Sea.

Crucified

I cried to men, "I would be crucified!"

And they said, "Why should your blood be upon our heads?"

And I answered, "How else shall you be exalted except by crucifying madmen?"

And they heeded and I was crucified. And the crucifixion appeased me.

And when I was hanged between earth and heaven they lifted up their heads to see me. And they were exalted, for their heads had never before been lifted.

But as they stood looking up at me one called out, "For what art thou seeking atone?"

And another cried, "In what cause dost thou sacrifice thyself?"

And a third said, "Thinkest thou with this price to buy world glory?"

Then said a fourth, "Behold, how he smiles! Can such pain be forgiven?"

And I answered them all, and said:

"Remember only that I smiled. I do not atone—nor sacrifice—nor wish for glory; and I have nothing to forgive. I thirsted—and I besought you to give me my blood to drink. For what is there can quench a madman's thirst but his own blood? I was dumb—and I asked wounds of you for mouths. I was imprisoned on your days and nights—and I sought a door into larger days and nights.

And now I go—as others already crucified have gone. And think not we are weary of crucifixion. For we must be crucified by larger and yet larger men, between greater earths and greater heavens."

The Astronomer

In the shadow of the temple my friend and I saw a blind man sitting alone. And my friend said, "Behold the wisest man of our land."

Then I left my friend and approached the blind man and greeted him. And we conversed.

After a while I said, "Forgive my question, but since when hast thou been blind?"

"From my birth," he answered.

Said I, "And what path of wisdom followest thou?"

Said he, "I am an astronomer."

Then he placed his hand upon his breast, saying, "I watch all these suns and moons and stars."

The Great Longing

Here I sit between my brother the mountain and my sister the sea.

We three are one in loneliness, and the love that binds us together is deep and strong and strange. Nay, it is deeper than my sister's depth and stronger than my brother's strength, and stranger than the strangeness of my madness.

Aeons upon aeons have passed since the first grey dawn made us visible to one another; and though we have seen the birth and the fullness and the death of many worlds, we are still eager and young. We are young and eager and yet we are mateless and unvisited, and though we lie in unbroken half embrace, we are uncomforted. And what comfort is there for controlled desire and unspent passion? Whence shall come the flaming god to warm my sister's bed? And what she-torrent shall quench my brother's fire? And who is the woman that shall command my heart?

In the stillness of the night my sister murmurs in her sleep the fire-god's unknown name, and my brother calls afar upon the cool and distant goddess. But upon whom I call in my sleep I know not.

Here I sit between my brother the mountain and my sister the sea. We three are one in loneliness, and the love that binds us together is deep and strong and strange.

Said A Blade Of Grass

Said a blade of grass to an autumn leaf, "You make such a noise falling! You scatter all my winter dreams."

Said the leaf indignant, "Low-born and low-dwelling! Songless, peevish thing! You live not in the upper air and you cannot tell the sound of singing."

Then the autumn leaf lay down upon the earth and slept. And when spring came she waked again—and she was a blade of grass.

And when it was autumn and her winter sleep was upon her, and above her through all the air the leaves were falling, she muttered to herself, "O these autumn leaves! They make such a noise! They scatter all my winter dreams."

The Eye

Said the Eye one day, "I see beyond these valleys a mountain veiled with blue mist. Is it not beautiful?"

The Ear listened, and after listening intently awhile, said, "But where is any mountain? I do not hear."

Then the Hand spoke and said, "I am trying in vain to feel it or touch it, and I can find no mountain."

And the Nose said, "There is no mountain, I cannot smell it."

Then the Eye turned the other way, and they all began to talk together about the Eye's strange delusion. And they said, "Something must be the matter with the Eye."

The Two Learned Men

Once there lived in the ancient city of Afkar two learned men who hated and belittled each other's learning. For one of them denied the existence of the gods and the other was a believer. One day the two met in the market-place, and amidst their followers they began to dispute and to argue about the existence or the non-existence of the gods. And after hours of contention they parted. That evening the unbeliever went to the temple and prostrated himself before the altar and prayed the gods to forgive his wayward past. And the same hour the other learned man, he who had upheld the gods, burned his sacred books. For he had become an unbeliever.

When My Sorrow Was Born

When my sorrow was born I nursed it with care, and watched over it with loving tenderness.

And my Sorrow grew like all living things, strong and beautiful and full of wondrous delights.

And we loved one another, my Sorrow and I, and we loved the world about us; for Sorrow had a kindly heart and mine was kindly with Sorrow.

And when we conversed, my Sorrow and I, our days were winged and our nights were girdled with dreams; for Sorrow had an eloquent tongue, and mine was eloquent with Sorrow.

And when we sang together, my Sorrow and I, our neighbors sat at their windows and listened; for our songs were deep as the sea and our melodies were full of strange memories.

And when we walked together, my Sorrow and I, people gazed at us with gentle eyes and whispered in words of exceeding sweetness. And there were those who looked with envy upon us, for Sorrow was a noble thing and I was proud with Sorrow.

But my Sorrow died, like all living things, and alone I am left to muse and ponder.

And now when I speak my words fall heavily upon my ears.

And when I sing my songs my neighbors come not to listen.

And when I walk the streets no one looks at me.

Only in my sleep I hear voices saying in pity, "See, there lies the man whose Sorrow is dead."

And When My Joy Was Born

And when my joy was born I held it in my arms and stood on the house-top shouting, "Come ye, my neighbors, come and see, for Joy this day is born unto me. Come and behold this gladsome thing that laugheth in the sun."

But none of my neighbors came to look upon my Joy, and great was my astonishment.

And every day for seven moons I proclaimed my Joy from the house-top—and yet no one heeded me. And my Joy and I were alone, unsought and unvisited.

Then my Joy grew pale and weary because no other heart but mine held its loveliness and no other lips kissed its lips.

Then my Joy died of isolation.

And now I only remember my dead Joy in remembering my dead Sorrow. But memory is an autumn leaf that murmurs in the wind and then is heard no more.

"The Perfect World"

God of lost souls, thou who art lost amongst the gods, hear me:

Gentle Destiny that watchest over us, mad, wandering spirits, hear me:

I dwell in the midst of a perfect race, I the most imperfect.

I, a human chaos, a nebula of confused elements, I move amongst finished worlds—peoples of complete laws and pure order, whose thoughts are assorted, whose dreams are arranged, and whose visions are enrolled and registered.

Their virtues, O God, are measured, their sins are weighed, and even the countless things that pass in the dim twilight of neither sin nor virtue are recorded and catalogued.

Here days and nights are divided into seasons of conduct and governed by rules of blameless accuracy.

To eat, to drink, to sleep, to cover one's nudity, and then to be weary in due time.

To work, to play, to sing, to dance, and then to lie still when the clock strikes the hour.

To think thus, to feel thus much, and then to cease thinking and feeling when a certain star rises above yonder horizon.

To rob a neighbor with a smile, to bestow gifts with a graceful wave of the hand, to praise prudently, to blame cautiously, to destroy a soul with a word, to burn a body with a breath, and then to wash the hands when the day's work is done.

To love according to an established order, to entertain one's best self in a pre-conceived manner, to worship the gods becomingly, to intrigue the devils artfully—and then to forget all as though memory were dead.

To fancy with a motive, to contemplate with consideration, to be happy sweetly, to suffer nobly—and then to empty the cup so that tomorrow may fill it again.

All these things, O God, are conceived with forethought, born with determination, nursed with exactness, governed by rules, directed by reason, and then slain and buried after a prescribed method. And even their silent graves that lie within the human soul are marked and numbered.

It is a perfect world, a world of consummate excellence, a world of supreme wonders, the ripest fruit in God's garden, the master-thought of the universe.

But why should I be here, O God, I a green seed of unfulfilled passion, a mad tempest that seeketh neither east nor west, a bewildered fragment from a burnt planet?

Why am I here, O God of lost souls, thou who art lost amongst the gods?

Sand And Foam

1926

I am forever walking upon these shores,
Betwixt the sand and the foam,
The high tide will erase my foot-prints,
And the wind will blow away the foam.
But the sea and the shore will remain
Forever.
Once I filled my hand with mist.
Then I opened it and lo, the mist was a worm.
And I closed and opened my hand again, and behold there was a bird.

And again I closed and opened my hand, and in its hollow stood a man with a sad face, turned upward.

And again I closed my hand, and when I opened it there was naught but mist.

But I heard a song of exceeding sweetness.

It was but yesterday I thought myself a fragment quivering without rhythm in the sphere of life.

Now I know that I am the sphere, and all life in rhythmic fragments moves within me.

They say to me in their awakening, "You and the world you live in are but a grain of sand upon the infinite shore of an infinite sea."

And in my dream I say to them, "I am the infinite sea, and all worlds are but grains of sand upon my shore."

Only once have I been made mute. It was when a man asked me, "Who are you?"

The first thought of God was an angel.

The first word of God was a man.

We were fluttering, wandering, longing creatures a thousand thousand years before the sea and the wind in the forest gave us words.

Now how can we express the ancient of days in us with only the sounds of our yesterdays?

The Sphinx spoke only once, and the Sphinx said, "A grain of sand is a desert, and a desert is a grain of sand; and now let us all be silent again."

I heard the Sphinx, but I did not understand.

Long did I lie in the dust of Egypt, silent and unaware of the seasons.

Then the sun gave me birth, and I rose and walked upon the banks of the Nile,

Singing with the days and dreaming with the nights.

And now the sun threads upon me with a thousand feet that I may lie again in the dust of Egypt.

But behold a marvel and a riddle!

The very sun that gathered me cannot scatter me.

Still erect am I, and sure of foot do I walk upon the banks of the Nile.

Remembrance is a form of meeting.

Forgetfulness is a form of freedom.

We measure time according to the movement of countless suns; and they measure time by little machines in their little pockets.

Now tell me, how could we ever meet at the same place and the same time?

Space is not space between the earth and the sun to one who looks down from the windows of the Milky Way.

Humanity is a river of light running from the ex-eternity to eternity.

Do not the spirits who dwell in the ether envy man his pain?

On my way to the Holy City I met another pilgrim and I asked him, "Is this indeed the way to the Holy City?"

And he said, "Follow me, and you will reach the Holy City in a day and a night."

And I followed him. And we walked many days and many nights, yet we did not reach the Holy City.

And what was to my surprise he became angry with me because he had misled me.

Make me, oh God, the prey of the lion, ere You make the rabbit my prey.

One may not reach the dawn save by the path of the night.

My house says to me, "Do not leave me, for here dwells your past."

And the road says to me, "Come and follow me, for I am your future."

And I say to both my house and the road, "I have no past, nor have I a future. If I stay here, there is a going in my staying; and if I go there is a staying in my going. Only love and death will change all things."

How can I lose faith in the justice of life, when the dreams of those who sleep upon feathers are not more beautiful than the dreams of those who sleep upon the earth?

Strange, the desire for certain pleasures is a part of my pain.

Seven times have I despised my soul:

The first time when I saw her being meek that she might attain height.

The second time when I saw her limping before the crippled.

The third time when she was given to choose between the hard and the easy, and she chose the easy.

The fourth time when she committed a wrong, and comforted herself that others also commit wrong.

The fifth time when she forbore for weakness, and attributed her patience to strength.

The sixth time when she despised the ugliness of a face, and knew not that it was one of her own masks.

And the seventh time when she sang a song of praise, and deemed it a virtue.

I am ignorant of absolute truth. But I am humble before my ignorance and therein lies my honor and my reward.

There is a space between man's imagination and man's attainment that may only be traversed by his longing.

Paradise is there, behind that door, in the next room; but I have lost the key.

Perhaps I have only mislaid it.

You are blind and I am deaf and dumb, so let us touch hands and understand.

The significance of man is not in what he attains, but rather in what he longs to attain.

Some of us are like ink and some like paper.

And if it were not for the blackness of some of us, some of us would be dumb;

And if it were not for the whiteness of some of us, some of us would be blind.

Give me an ear and I will give you a voice.

Our mind is a sponge; our heart is a stream.

Is it not strange that most of us choose sucking rather than running?

When you long for blessings that you may not name, and when you grieve knowing not the cause, then indeed you are growing with all things that grow, and rising toward your greater self.

When one is drunk with a vision, he deems his faint expression of it the very wine.

You drink wine that you may be intoxicated; and I drink that it may sober me from that other wine.

When my cup is empty I resign myself to its emptiness; but when it is half full I resent its half-fulness.

The reality of the other person is not in what he reveals to you, but in what he cannot reveal to you.

Therefore, if you would understand him, listen not to what he says but rather to what he does not say.

Half of what I say is meaningless; but I say it so that the other half may reach you.

A sense of humor is a sense of proportion.

My loneliness was born when men praised my talkative faults and blamed my silent virtues.

When Life does not find a singer to sing her heart she produces a philosopher to speak her mind.

A truth is to be known always, to be uttered sometimes.

The real in us is silent; the acquired is talkative.

The voice of life in me cannot reach the ear of life in you; but let us talk that we may not feel lonely.

When two women talk they say nothing; when one woman speaks she reveals all of life.

Frogs may bellow louder than bulls, but they cannot drag the plough in the field not turn the wheel of the winepress, and of their skins you cannot make shoes.

Only the dumb envy the talkative.

If winter should say, "Spring is in my heart," who would believe winter?

Every seed is a longing.

Should you really open your eyes and see, you would behold your image in all images.

And should you open your ears and listen, you would hear your own voice in all voices.

It takes two of us to discover truth: one to utter it and one to understand it.

Though the wave of words is forever upon us, yet our depth is forever silent.

Many a doctrine is like a window pane. We see truth through it but it divides us from truth.

Now let us play hide and seek. Should you hide in my heart it would not be difficult to find you. But should you hide behind your own shell, then it would be useless for anyone to seek you.

A woman may veil her face with a smile.

How noble is the sad heart who would sing a joyous song with joyous hearts.

He who would understand a woman, or dissect genius, or solve the mystery of silence is the very man who would wake from a beautiful dream to sit at a breakfast table.

I would walk with all those who walk. I would not stand still to watch the procession passing by.

You owe more than gold to him who serves you. Give him of your heart or serve him.

Nay, we have not lived in vain. Have they not built towers of our bones?

Let us not be particular and sectional. The poet's mind and the scorpion's tail rise in glory from the same earth.

Every dragon gives birth to a St. George who slays it.

Trees are poems that the earth writes upon the sky. We fell them down and turn them into paper that we may record our emptiness.

Should you care to write (and only the saints know why you should) you must needs have knowledge and art and music — the knowledge of the music of words, the art of being artless, and the magic of loving your readers.

They dip their pens in our hearts and think they are inspired.

Should a tree write its autobiography it would not be unlike the history of a race.

If I were to choose between the power of writing a poem and the ecstasy of a poem unwritten, I would choose the ecstasy. It is better poetry.

But you and all my neighbors agree that I always choose badly.

Poetry is not an opinion expressed. It is a song that rises from a bleeding wound or a smiling mouth.

Words are timeless. You should utter them or write them with a knowledge of their timelessness.

A poet is a dethroned king sitting among the ashes of his palace trying to fashion an image out of the ashes.

Poetry is a deal of joy and pain and wonder, with a dash of the dictionary.

In vain shall a poet seek the mother of the songs of his heart.

Once I said to a poet, "We shall not know your worth until you die."

And he answered saying, "Yes, death is always the revealer. And if indeed you would know my worth it is that I have more in my heart than upon my tongue, and more in my desire than in my hand."

If you sing of beauty though alone in the heart of the desert you will have an audience.

Poetry is wisdom that enchants the heart.

Wisdom is poetry that sings in the mind.

If we could enchant man's heart and at the same time sing in his mind,

Then in truth he would live in the shadow of God.

Inspiration will always sing; inspiration will never explain.

We often sing lullabies to our children that we ourselves may sleep.

All our words are but crumbs that fall down from the feast of the mind.

Thinking is always the stumbling stone to poetry.

A great singer is he who sings our silences.

How can you sing if your mouth be filled with food?

How shall your hand be raised in blessing if it is filled with gold?

They say the nightingale pierces his bosom with a thorn when he sings his love song.

So do we all. How else should we sing?

Genius is but a robin's song at the beginning of a slow spring.

Even the most winged spirit cannot escape physical necessity.

A madman is not less a musician than you or myself; only the instrument on which he plays is a little out of tune.

The song that lies silent in the heart of a mother sings upon the lips of her child.

No longing remains unfulfilled.

I have never agreed with my other self wholly. The truth of the matter seems to lie between us.

Your other self is always sorry for you. But your other self grows on sorrow; so all is well.

There is no struggle of soul and body save in the minds of those whose souls are asleep and whose bodies are out of tune.

When you reach the heart of life you shall find beauty in all things, even in the eyes that are blind to beauty.

We live only to discover beauty. All else is a form of waiting.

Sow a seed and the earth will yield you a flower. Dream your dream to the sky and it will bring you your beloved.

The devil died the very day you were born.

Now you do not have to go through hell to meet an angel.

Many a woman borrows a man's heart; very few could possess it.

If you would possess you must not claim.

When a man's hand touches the hand of a woman they both touch the heart of eternity.

Love is the veil between lover and lover.

Every man loves two women; the one is the creation of his imagination, and the other is not yet born.

Men who do not forgive women their little faults will never enjoy their great virtues.

Love that does not renew itself every day becomes a habit and in turn a slavery.

Lovers embrace that which is between them rather than each other.

Love and doubt have never been on speaking terms.

Love is a word of light, written by a hand of light, upon a page of light.

Friendship is always a sweet responsibility, never an opportunity.

If you do not understand your friend under all conditions you will never understand him.

Your most radiant garment is of the other person's weaving;

You most savory meal is that which you eat at the other person's table;

Your most comfortable bed is in the other person's house.

Now tell me, how can you separate yourself from the other person?

Your mind and my heart will never agree until your mind ceases to live in numbers and my heart in the mist.

We shall never understand one another until we reduce the language to seven words.

How shall my heart be unsealed unless it be broken?

Only great sorrow or great joy can reveal your truth.

If you would be revealed you must either dance naked in the sun, or carry your cross.

Should nature heed what we say of contentment no river would seek the sea, and no winter would turn to Spring. Should she heed all we say of thrift, how many of us would be breathing this air?

You see but your shadow when you turn your back to the sun.

You are free before the sun of the day, and free before the stars of the night;

And you are free when there is no sun and no moon and no star.

You are even free when you close your eyes upon all there is.

But you are a slave to him whom you love because you love him,

And a slave to him who loves you because he loves you.

We are all beggars at the gate of the temple, and each one of us receives his share of the bounty of the King when he enters the temple, and when he goes out.

But we are all jealous of one another, which is another way of belittling the King.

You cannot consume beyond your appetite. The other half of the loaf belongs to the other person, and there should remain a little bread for the chance guest.

If it were not for your guests all houses would be graves.

Said a gracious wolf to a simple sheep, "Will you not honor our house with a visit?"

And the sheep answered, "We would have been honored to visit your house if it were not in your stomach."

I stopped my guest on the threshold and said, "Nay, wipe not your feet as you enter, but as you go out."

Generosity is not in giving me that which I need more than you do, but it is in giving me that which you need more than I do.

You are indeed charitable when you give, and while giving, turn your face away so that you may not see the shyness of the receiver.

The difference between the richest man and the poorest is but a day of hunger and an hour of thirst.

We often borrow from our tomorrows to pay our debts to our yesterdays.

I too am visited by angels and devils, but I get rid of them.

When it is an angel I pray an old prayer, and he is bored;

When it is a devil I commit an old sin, and he passes me by.

After all this is not a bad prison; but I do not like this wall between my cell and the next prisoner's cell;

Yet I assure you that I do not wish to reproach the warder not the Builder of the prison.

Those who give you a serpent when you ask for a fish, may have nothing but serpents to give. It is then generosity on their part.

Trickery succeeds sometimes, but it always commits suicide.

You are truly a forgiver when you forgive murderers who never spill blood, thieves who never steal, and liars who utter no falsehood.

He who can put his finger upon that which divides good from evil is he who can touch the very hem of the garment of God.

If your heart is a volcano how shall you expect flowers to bloom in your hands?

A strange form of self-indulgence! There are times when I would be wronged and cheated, that I may laugh at the expense of those who think I do not know I am being wronged and cheated.

What shall I say of him who is the pursuer playing the part of the pursued?

Let him who wipes his soiled hands with your garment take your garment. He may need it again; surely you would not.

It is a pity that money-changers cannot be good gardeners.

Please do not whitewash your inherent faults with your acquired virtues. I would have the faults; they are like mine own.

How often have I attributed to myself crimes I have never committed, so that the other person may feel comfortable in my presence.

Even the masks of life are masks of deeper mystery.

You may judge others only according to your knowledge of yourself.

Tell me now, who among us is guilty and who is unguilty?

The truly just is he who feels half guilty of your misdeeds.

Only an idiot and a genius break man-made laws; and they are the nearest to the heart of God.

It is only when you are pursued that you become swift.

I have no enemies, O God, but if I am to have an enemy

Let his strength be equal to mine,

That truth alone may be the victor.

You will be quite friendly with your enemy when you both die.

Perhaps a man may commit suicide in self-defense.

Long ago there lived a Man who was crucified for being too loving and too lovable.

And strange to relate I met him thrice yesterday.

The first time He was asking a policeman not to take a prostitute to prison; the second time He was drinking wine with an outcast; and the third time He was having a fist-fight with a promoter inside a church.

If all they say of good and evil were true, then my life is but one long crime.

Pity is but half justice.

The only one who has been unjust to me is the one to whose brother I have been unjust.

When you see a man led to prison say in your heart, "Mayhap he is escaping from a narrower prison."

And when you see a man drunken say in your heart, "Mayhap he sought escape from something still more unbeautiful."

Oftentimes I have hated in self-defense; but if I were stronger I would not have used such a weapon.

How stupid is he who would patch the hatred in his eyes with the smile of his lips.

Only those beneath me can envy or hate me.

I have never been envied nor hated; I am above no one.

Only those above me can praise or belittle me.

I have never been praised nor belittled; I am below no one.

Your saying to me, "I do not understand you," is praise beyond my worth, and an insult you do not deserve.

How mean am I when life gives me gold and I give you silver, and yet I deem myself generous.

When you reach the heart of life you will find yourself not higher than the felon, and not lower than the prophet.

Strange that you should pity the slow-footed and not the slow-minded,

And the blind-eyed rather than the blind-hearted.

It is wiser for the lame not to break his crutches upon the head of his enemy.

How blind is he who gives you out of his pocket that he may take out of your heart.

Life is a procession. The slow of foot finds it too swift and he steps out;

And the swift of foot finds it too slow and he too steps out.

If there is such a thing as sin some of us commit it backward following our forefathers' footsteps;

And some of us commit it forward by overruling our children.

The truly good is he who is one with all those who are deemed bad.

We are all prisoners but some of us are in cells with windows and some without.

Strange that we all defend our wrongs with more vigor than we do our rights.

Should we all confess our sins to one another we would all laugh at one another for our lack of originality.

Should we all reveal our virtues we would also laugh for the same cause.

An individual is above man-made laws until he commits a crime against man-made conventions; After that he is neither above anyone nor lower than anyone.

Government is an agreement between you and myself. You and myself are often wrong.

Crime is either another name of need or an aspect of a disease.

Is there a greater fault than being conscious of the other person's faults?

If the other person laughs at you, you can pity him; but if you laugh at him you may never forgive yourself.

If the other person injures you, you may forget the injury; but if you injure him you will always remember.

In truth the other person is your most sensitive self given another body.

How heedless you are when you would have men fly with your wings and you cannot even give them a feather.

Once a man sat at my board and ate my bread and drank my wine and went away laughing at me.

Then he came again for bread and wine, and I spurned him;

And the angels laughed at me.

Hate is a dead thing. Who of you would be a tomb?

It is the honor of the murdered that he is not the murderer.

The tribune of humanity is in its silent heart, never its talkative mind.

They deem me mad because I will not sell my days for gold;

And I deem them mad because they think my days have a price.

They spread before us their riches of gold and silver, of ivory and ebony, and we spread before them our hearts and our spirits.;

And yet they deem themselves the hosts and us the guests.

I would not be the least among men with dreams and the desire to fulfill them, rather than the greatest with no dreams and no desires.

The most pitiful among men is he who turns his dreams into silver and gold.

We are all climbing toward the summit of our hearts' desire. Should the other climber steal your sack and your purse and wax fat on the one and heavy on the other, you should pity him;

The climbing will be harder for his flesh, and the burden will make his way longer.

And should you in your leanness see his flesh puffing upward, help him a step; it will add to your swiftness.

You cannot judge any man beyond your knowledge of him, and how small is your knowledge.

I would not listen to a conqueror preaching to the conquered.

The truly free man is he who bears the load of the bond slave patiently.

A thousand years ago my neighbor said to me, "I hate life, for it is naught but a thing of pain."

And yesterday I passed by a cemetery and saw life dancing upon his grave.

Strife in nature is but disorder longing for order.

Solitude is a silent storm that breaks down all our dead branches;

Yet it sends our living roots deeper into the living heart of the living earth.

Once I spoke of the sea to a brook, and the brook thought me but an imaginative exaggerator;

And once I spoke of a brook to the sea, and the sea thought me but a depreciative defamer.

How narrow is the vision that exalts the busyness of the ant above the singing of the grasshopper.

The highest virtue here may be the least in another world.

The deep and the high go to the depth or to the height in a straight line; only the spacious can move in circles.

If it were not for our conception of weights and measures we would stand in awe of the firefly as we do before the sun.

A scientist without imagination is a butcher with dull knives and out-worn scales.

But what would you, since we are not all vegetarians?

When you sing the hungry hears you with his stomach.

Death is not nearer to the aged than to the new-born; neither is life.

If indeed you must be candid, be candid beautifully; otherwise keep silent, for there is a man in our neighborhood who is dying.

Mayhap a funeral among men is a wedding feast among the angels.

A forgotten reality may die and leave in its will seven thousand actualities and facts to be spent in its funeral and the building of a tomb.

In truth we talk only to ourselves, but sometimes we talk loud enough that others may hear us.

The obvious is that which is never seen until someone expresses it simply.

If the Milky Way were not within me how should I have seen it or known it?

Unless I am a physician among physicians they would not believe that I am an astronomer.

Perhaps the sea's definition of a shell is the pearl.

Perhaps time's definition of coal is the diamond.

Fame is the shadow of passion standing in the light.

A root is a flower that disdains fame.

There is neither religion nor science beyond beauty.

Every great man I have known had something small in his make-up; and it was that small something which prevented inactivity or madness or suicide.

The truly great man is he who would master no one, and who would be mastered by none.

I would not believe that a man is mediocre simply because he kills the criminals and the prophets.

Tolerance is love sick with the sickness of haughtiness.

Worms will turn; but is it not strange that even elephants will yield?

A disagreement may be the shortest cut between two minds.

I am the flame and I am the dry bush, and one part of me consumes the other part.

We are all seeking the summit of the holy mountain; but shall not our road be shorter if we consider the past a chart and not a guide?

Wisdom ceases to be wisdom when it becomes too proud to weep, too grave to laugh, and too self-full to seek other than itself.

Had I filled myself with all that you know what room should I have for all that you do not know?

I have learned silence from the talkative, toleration from the intolerant, and kindness from the unkind; yet strange, I am ungrateful to these teachers.

A bigot is a stone-leaf orator.

The silence of the envious is too noisy.

When you reach the end of what you should know, you will be at the beginning of what you should sense.

An exaggeration is a truth that has lost its temper.

If you can see only what light reveals and hear only what sound announces,

Then in truth you do not see nor do you hear.

A fact is a truth unsexed.

You cannot laugh and be unkind at the same time.

The nearest to my heart are a king without a kingdom and a poor man who does not know how to beg.

A shy failure is nobler than an immodest success.

Dig anywhere in the earth and you will find a treasure, only you must dig with the faith of a peasant.

Said a hunted fox followed by twenty horsemen and a pack of twenty hounds, "Of course they will kill me. But how poor and how stupid they must be. Surely it would not be worthwhile for twenty foxes riding on twenty asses and accompanied by twenty wolves to chase and kill one man."

It is the mind in us that yields to the laws made by us, but never the spirit in us.

A traveler am I and a navigator, and every day I discover a new region within my soul.

A woman protested saying, "Of course it was a righteous war. My son fell in it."

I said to Life, "I would hear Death speak."

And Life raised her voice a little higher and said, "You hear him now."

When you have solved all the mysteries of life you long for death, for it is but another mystery of life.

Birth and death are the two noblest expressions of bravery.

My friend, you and I shall remain strangers unto life,
And unto one another, and each unto himself,
Until the day when you shall speak and I shall listen
Deeming your voice my own voice;
And when I shall stand before you
Thinking myself standing before a mirror.

They say to me, "Should you know yourself you would know all men."

And I say, "Only when I seek all men shall I know myself."

Man is two men; one is awake in darkness, the other is asleep in light.

A hermit is one who renounces the world of fragments that he may enjoy the world wholly and without interruption.

There lies a green field between the scholar and the poet; should the scholar cross it he becomes a wise man; should the poet cross it, he becomes a prophet.

Yestereve I saw philosophers in the market-place carrying their heads in baskets, and crying aloud, "Wisdom! Wisdom for sale!"

Poor philosophers! They must needs sell their heads to feed their hearts.

Said a philosopher to a street sweeper, "I pity you. Yours is a hard and dirty task."

And the street sweeper said, "Thank you, sir. But tell me what is your task?"

And the philosopher answered saying, "I study man's mind, his deeds and his desires."

Then the street sweeper went on with his sweeping and said with a smile, "I pity you too."

He who listens to truth is not less than he who utters truth.

No man can draw the line between necessities and luxuries. Only the angels can do that, and the angels are wise and wistful.

Perhaps the angels are our better thought in space.

He is the true prince who finds his throne in the heart of the dervish.

Generosity is giving more than you can, and pride is taking less than you need.

In truth you owe naught to any man. You owe all to all men.

All those who have lived in the past live with us now. Surely none of us would be an ungracious host.

He who longs the most lives the longest.

They say to me, "A bird in the hand is worth ten in the bush."

But I say, "A bird and a feather in the bush is worth more than ten birds in the hand."

Your seeking after that feather is life with winged feet; nay, it is life itself.

There are only two elements here, beauty and truth; beauty in the hearts of lovers, and truth in the arms of the tillers of the soil.

Great beauty captures me, but a beauty still greater frees me even from itself.

Beauty shines brighter in the heart of him who longs for it than in the eyes of him who sees it.

I admire him who reveals his mind to me; I honor him who unveils his dreams. But why am I shy, and even a little ashamed before him who serves me?

The gifted were once proud in serving princes.

Now they claim honor in serving paupers.

The angels know that too many practical men eat their bread with the sweat of the dreamer's brow.

Wit is often a mask. If you could tear it you would find either a genius irritated or cleverness juggling.

The understanding attributes to me understanding and the dull, dullness. I think they are both right.

Only those with secrets in their hearts could divine the secrets in our hearts.

He who would share your pleasure but not your pain shall lose the key to one of the seven gates of Paradise.

Yes, there is a Nirvana; it is in leading your sheep to a green pasture, and in putting your child to sleep, and in writing the last line of your poem.

We choose our joys and our sorrows long before we experience them.

Sadness is but a wall between two gardens.

When either your joy or your sorrow becomes great the world becomes small.

Desire is half of life; indifference is half of death.

The bitterest thing in our today's sorrow is the memory of our yesterday's joy.

They say to me, "You must needs choose between the pleasures of this world and the peace of the next world."

And I say to them, "I have chosen both the delights of this world and the peace of the next. For I know in my heart that the Supreme Poet wrote but one poem, and it scans perfectly, and it also rhymes perfectly."

Faith is an oasis in the heart which will never be reached by the caravan of thinking.

When you reach your height you shall desire but only for desire; and you shall hunger, for hunger; and you shall thirst for greater thirst.

If you reveal your secrets to the wind you should not blame the wind for revealing them to the trees.

The flowers of spring are winter's dreams related at the breakfast table of the angels.

Said a skunk to a tube-rose, "See how swiftly I run, while you cannot walk nor even creep."

Said the tube-rose to the skunk, "Oh, most noble swift runner, please run swiftly!"

Turtles can tell more about roads than hares.

Strange that creatures without backbones have the hardest shells.

The most talkative is the least intelligent, and there is hardly a difference between an orator and an auctioneer.

Be grateful that you do not have to live down the renown of a father nor the wealth of an uncle.

But above all be grateful that no one will have to live down either your renown or your wealth.

Only when a juggler misses catching his ball does he appeal to me.

The envious praises me unknowingly.

Long were you a dream in your mother's sleep, and then she woke to give you birth.

The germ of the race is in your mother's longing.

My father and mother desired a child and they begot me.

And I wanted a mother and a father and I begot night and the sea.

Some of our children are our justifications and some are but our regrets.

When night comes and you too are dark, lie down and be dark with a will.

And when morning comes and you are still dark stand up and say to the day with a will, "I am still dark."

It is stupid to play a role with the night and the day.

They would both laugh at you.

The Forerunner
1920

The Forerunner

You are your own forerunner, and the towers you have built are but the foundation of your giant-self. And that self too shall be a foundation.

And I too am my own forerunner, for the long shadow stretching before me at sunrise shall gather under my feet at the noon hour. Yet another sunrise shall lay another shadow before me, and that also shall be gathered at another noon.

Always have we been our own forerunners, and always shall we be. And all that we have gathered and shall gather shall be but seeds for fields yet unplowed. We are the fields and the plowmen, the gatherers and the gathered.

When you were a wandering desire in the mist, I too was there, a wandering desire. Then we sought one another, and out of our eagerness dreams were born. And dreams were time limitless, and dreams were space without measure.

And when you were a silent word upon life's quivering lips, I too was there, another silent word. Then life uttered us and we came down the years throbbing with memories of yesterday and with longing for tomorrow, for yesterday was death conquered and tomorrow was birth pursued.

And now we are in God's hands. You are a sun in His right hand and I an earth in His left hand. Yet you are not more, shining, than I, shone upon.

And we, sun and earth, are but the beginning of a greater sun and a greater earth. And always shall we be the beginning.

You are your own forerunner, you the stranger passing by the gate of my garden.

And I too am my own forerunner, though I sit in the shadows of my trees and seem motionless.

God's Fool

Once there came from the desert to the great city of Sharia a man who was a dreamer, and he had naught but his garment and staff.

And as he walked through the streets he gazed with awe and wonder at the temples and towers and palaces, for the city of Sharia was of surpassing beauty. And he spoke often to the passers-by, questioning them about their city - but they understood not his language, nor he their language.

At the noon hour he stopped before a vast inn. It was built of yellow marble, and people were going in and coming out unhindered.

"This must be a shrine," he said to himself, and he too went in. But what was his surprise to find himself in a hall of great splendor and a large company of men and women seated about many tables. They were eating and drinking and listening to the musicians.

"Nay," said the dreamer. "This is no worshipping. It must be a feast given by the prince to the people, in celebration of a great event."

At that moment a man, whom he took to be the slave of the prince, approached him, and bade him be seated. And he was served with meat and wine and most excellent sweets.

When he was satisfied, the dreamer rose to depart. At the door he was stopped by a large man magnificently arrayed.

"Surely this is the prince himself," said the dreamer in his heart, and he bowed to him and thanked him.

Then the large man said in the language of the city:

"Sir, you have not paid for your dinner." And the dreamer did not understand, and again thanked him heartily. Then the large man bethought him, and he looked more closely upon the dreamer. And he saw that he was a stranger, clad in but a poor garment, and that indeed he had not wherewith to pay for his meal. Then the large man clapped his hands and called - and there came four watchmen of the city. And they listened to the large man. Then they took the dreamer between them, and they were two on each side of him. And the dreamer noted the ceremoniousness of their dress and of their manner and he looked upon them with delight. "These," said he, "are men of distinction."

And they walked all together until they came to the House of Judgment and they entered.

The dreamer saw before him, seated upon a throne, a venerable man with flowing beard, robed majestically. And he thought he was the king. And he rejoiced to be brought before him.

Now the watchmen related to the judge, who was the venerable man, the charge against the dreamer, and the judge appointed two advocates, one to present the charge and the other to defend the stranger. And the advocates rose, the one after the other, and delivered each his argument. And the dreamer thought himself to be listening to addresses of welcome, and his heart filled with gratitude to the king and the prince for all that was done for him.

Then sentence was passed upon the dreamer, that upon a tablet about his neck his crime should be written, and that he should ride through the city on a naked horse, with a trumpeter and a drummer before him. And the sentence was carried out forthwith.

Now as the dreamer rode through the city upon the naked horse, with the trumpeter and the drummer before him, the inhabitants of the city came running forth at the sound of the noise, and when they saw him they laughed one and all, and the children ran after him in companies from street to street. And the dreamer's heart was filled with ecstasy, and his eyes shone upon them. For to him the tablet was a sign of the king's blessing and the procession was in his honor.

Now as he rode, he saw among the crowd a man who was from the desert like himself and his heart swelled with joy, and he cried out to him with a shout:

"Friend! Friend! Where are we? What city of the heart's desire is this? What race of lavish hosts, who feast the chance guest in their palaces, whose princes companion him, whose kings hangs a token upon his breast and opens to him the hospitality of a city descended from heaven?"

And he who was also of the desert replied not. He only smiled and slightly shook his head. And the procession passed on.

And the dreamer's face was uplifted and his eyes were overflowing with light.

Love

They say the jackal and the mole
Drink from the selfsame stream
Where the lion comes to drink.
And they say the eagle and the vulture
Dig their beaks into the same carcass,
And are at peace, one with the other,
In the presence of the dead thing.
O love, whose lordly hand
Has bridled my desires,
And raised my hunger and my thirst
To dignity and pride,
Let not the strong in me and the constant
Eat the bread or drink the wine
That tempt my weaker self.
Let me rather starve,
And let my heart parch with thirst,
And let me die and perish,
Ere I stretch my hand
To a cup you did not fill,
Or a bowl you did not bless.

The King-Hermit

They told me that in a forest among the mountains lives a young man in solitude who once was a king of a vast country beyond the Two Rivers. And they also said that he, of his own will, had left his throne and the land of his glory and come to dwell in the wilderness.

And I said, "I would seek that man, and learn the secret of his heart; for he who renounces a kingdom must needs be greater than a kingdom."

On that very day I went to the forest where he dwells. And I found him sitting under a white cypress, and in his hand a reed as if it were a scepter. And I greeted him even as I would greet a king. And he turned to me and said gently, "What would you in this forest of serenity? Seek you a lost self in the green shadows, or is it a home-coming in your twilight?"

And I answered, "I sought but you—for I fain would know that which made you leave a kingdom for a forest."

And he said, "Brief is my story, for sudden was the bursting of the bubble. It happened thus: one day as I sat at a window in my palace, my chamberlain and an envoy from a foreign land were walking in my garden. And as they approached my window, the lord chamberlain was speaking of himself and saying, 'I am like the king; I have a thirst for strong wine and a hunger for all games of chance. And like my lord the king I have storms of temper.' And the lord chamberlain and the envoy disappeared among the trees. But in a few minutes they returned, and this time the lord chamberlain was speaking of me, and he was saying, 'My lord the king is like myself—a good marksman; and like me he loves music and bathes thrice a day.' "

After a moment he added, "On the eve of that day I left my palace with but my garment, for I would no longer be ruler over those who assume my vices and attribute to me their virtues."

And I said, "This is indeed a wonder, and passing strange."

And he said, "Nay, my friend, you knocked at the gate of my silences and received but a trifle. For who would not leave a kingdom for a forest where the seasons sing and dance ceaselessly? Many are those who have given their kingdom for less than solitude and the sweet fellowship of aloneness. Countless are the eagles who descend from the upper air to live with moles that they may know the secrets of the earth. There are those who renounce the kingdom of dreams that they may not seem distant from the dreamless. And those who renounce the kingdom of nakedness and cover their souls that others may not be ashamed in beholding truth uncovered and beauty unveiled. And greater yet than all of these is he who renounces the kingdom of sorrow that he may not seem proud and vainglorious."

Then rising he leaned upon his reed and said, "Go now to the great city and sit at its gate and watch all those who enter into it and those who go out. And see that you find him who, though born a king, is without kingdom; and him who though ruled in flesh rules in spirit — though neither he nor his subjects know this; and him also who but seems to rule yet is in truth slave of his own slaves."

After he had said these things he smiled on me, and there were a thousand dawns upon his lips. Then he turned and walked away into the heart of the forest.

And I returned to the city, and I sat at its gate to watch the passers-by even as he had told me. And from that day to this numberless are the kings whose shadows have passed over me and few are the subjects over whom my shadow passed.

The Lion's Daughter

Four slaves stood fanning an old queen who was asleep upon her throne. And she was snoring. And upon the queen's lap a cat lay purring and gazing lazily at the slaves.

The first slave spoke, and said, "How ugly this old woman is in her sleep. See her mouth droop; and she breathes as if the devil were choking her."

Then the cat said, purring, "Not half so ugly in her sleep as you in your waking slavery."

And the second slave said, "You would think sleep would smooth her wrinkles instead of deepening them. She must be dreaming of something evil."

And the cat purred, "Would that you might sleep also and dream of your freedom."

And the third slave said, "Perhaps she is seeing the procession of all those that she has slain."

And the cat purred, "Aye, she sees the procession of your forefathers and your descendants."

And the fourth slave said, "It is all very well to talk about her, but it does not make me less weary of standing and fanning."

And the cat purred, "You shall be fanning to all eternity; for as it is on earth, so it is in heaven."

At this moment the old queen nodded in her sleep, and her crown fell to the floor.

And one of the slaves said, "That is a bad omen."

And the cat purred, "The bad omen of one is the good omen of another."

And the second slave said, "What if she should wake, and find her crown fallen! She would surely slay us."

And the cat purred, "Daily from your birth she has slain you and you know it not."

And the third slave said, "Yes, she would slay us and she would call it making a sacrifice to the gods."

And the cat purred, "Only the weak are sacrificed to the gods."

And the fourth slave silenced the others, and softly he picked up the crown and replaced it, without waking her, on the old queen's head.

And the cat purred, "Only a slave restores a crown that has fallen."

And after a while the old queen woke, and she looked about her and yawned. Then she said, "Methought I dreamed, and I saw four caterpillars chased by a scorpion around the trunk of an ancient oak tree. I like not my dream."

Then she closed her eyes and went to sleep again. And she snored. And the four slaves went on fanning her.

And the cat purred, "Fan on, fan on, stupids. You fan but the fire that consumes you."

Tyranny

Thus sings the she-dragon that guards the seven caves by the sea:

"My mate shall come riding on the waves. His thundering roar shall fill the earth with fear, and the flames of his nostrils shall set the sky afire. At the eclipse of the moon we shall be wedded, and at the eclipse of the sun I shall give birth to a Saint George, who shall slay me."

Thus sings the she-dragon that guards the seven caves by the sea.

The Saint

In my youth I once visited a saint in his silent grove beyond the hills; and as we were conversing upon the nature of virtue a brigand came limping wearily up the ridge. When he reached the grove he knelt down before the saint and said, "O saint, I would be comforted! My sins are heavy upon me."

And the saint replied, "My sins, too, are heavy upon me."

And the brigand said, "But I am a thief and a plunderer."

And the saint replied, "I too am a thief and a plunderer."

And the brigand said, "But I am a murderer, and the blood of many men cries in my ears."

And the saint replied, "I am a murderer, and in my ears cries the blood of many men."

And the brigand said, "I have committed countless crimes."

And the saint replied, "I too have committed crimes without number."

Then the brigand stood up and gazed at the saint, and there was a strange look in his eyes. And when he left us he went skipping down the hill.

And I turned to the saint and said, "Wherefore did you accuse yourself of uncommitted crimes? See you not this man went away no longer believing in you?"

And the saint answered, "It is true he no longer believes in me. But he went away much comforted."

At that moment we heard the brigand singing in the distance, and the echo of his song filled the valley with gladness.

The Plutocrat

In my wanderings I once saw upon an island a man-headed, iron-hoofed monster who ate of the earth and drank of the sea incessantly. And for a long while I watched him. Then I approached him and said, "Have you never enough; is your hunger never satisfied and your thirst never quenched?"

And he answered saying, "Yes, I am satisfied, nay, I am weary of eating and drinking; but I am afraid that tomorrow there will be no more earth to eat and no more sea to drink."

The Greater Self

This came to pass. After the coronation of Nufsibaal King of Byblus, he retired to his bed-chamber—the very room which the three hermit-magicians of the mountains had built for him. He took off his crown and his royal raiment, and stood in the center of the room thinking of himself, now the all-powerful ruler of Byblus.

Suddenly he turned; and he saw stepping out of the silver mirror which his mother had given him, a naked man.

The king was startled, and he cried out to the man, "What would you?"

And the naked man answered, "Naught but this: Why have they crowned you king?"

And the king answered, "Because I am the noblest man in the land."

Then the naked man said, "If you were still more noble, you would not be king."

And the king said, "Because I am the mightiest man in the land they crowned me."

And the naked man said, "If you were mightier yet, you would not be king."

Then the king said, "Because I am the wisest man they crowned me king."

And the naked man said, "If you were still wiser you would not choose to be king."

Then the king fell to the floor and wept bitterly.

The naked man looked down upon him. Then he took up the crown and with tenderness replaced it upon the king's bent head.

And the naked man, gazing lovingly upon the king, entered into the mirror.

And the king roused, and straightway he looked into the mirror. And he saw there but himself crowned.

War And The Small Nations

Once, high above a pasture, where a sheep and a lamb were grazing, an eagle was circling and gazing hungrily down upon the lamb. And as he was about to descend and seize his prey, another eagle appeared and hovered above the sheep and her young with the same hungry intent. Then the two rivals began to fight, filling the sky with their fierce cries.

The sheep looked up and was much astonished. She turned to the lamb and said:

"How strange, my child, that these two noble birds should attack one another. Is not the vast sky large enough for both of them? Pray, my little one, pray in your heart that God may make peace between your winged brothers."

And the lamb prayed in his heart.

Critics

One nightfall a man travelling on horseback towards the sea reached an inn by the roadside. He dismounted and, confident in man and night like all riders towards the sea, he tied his horse to a tree beside the door and entered into the inn.

At midnight, when all were asleep, a thief came and stole the traveler's horse.

In the morning the man awoke, and discovered that his horse was stolen. And he grieved for his horse, and that a man had found it in his heart to steal.

Then his fellow lodgers came and stood around him and began to talk.

And the first man said, "How foolish of you to tie your horse outside the stable."

And the second said, "Still more foolish, without even hobbling the horse!"

And the third man said, "It is stupid at best to travel to the sea on horseback."

And the fourth said, "Only the indolent and the slow of foot own horses."

Then the traveler was much astonished. At last he cried, "My friends, because my horse was stolen, you have hastened one and all to tell me my faults and my shortcomings. But strange, not one word of reproach have you uttered about the man who stole my horse."

Poets

Four poets were sitting around a bowl of punch that stood on a table.

Said the first poet, "Methinks I see with my third eye the fragrance of this wine hovering in space like a cloud of birds in an enchanted forest."

The second poet raised his head and said, "With my inner ear I can hear those mist-birds singing. And the melody holds my heart as the white rose imprisons the bee within her petals."

The third poet closed his eyes and stretched his arm upwards, and said, "I touch them with my hand. I feel their wings, like the breath of a sleeping fairy, brushing against my fingers."

Then the fourth poet rose and lifted up the bowl, and he said, "Alas, friends! I am too dull of sight and of hearing and of touch. I cannot see the fragrance of this wine, nor hear its song, nor feel the beating of its wings. I perceive but the wine itself. Now therefore must I drink it, that it may sharpen my senses and raise me to your blissful heights."

And putting the bowl to his lips, he drank the punch to the very last drop.

The three poets, with their mouths open, looked at him aghast, and there was a thirsty yet unlyrical hatred in their eyes.

The Weather-Cock

Said the weather-cock to the wind, "How tedious and monotonous you are! Can you not blow any other way

but in my face? You disturb my God-given stability."
And the wind did not answer. It only laughed in space.

The King of Aradus

Once the elders of the city of Aradus presented themselves before the king, and besought of him a decree to forbid to men all wine and all intoxicants within their city.

And the king turned his back upon them and went out from them laughing.

Then the elders departed in dismay.

At the door of the palace they met the lord chamberlain. And the lord chamberlain observed that they were troubled, and he understood their case.

Then he said, "Pity, my friends! Had you found the king drunk, surely he would have granted you your petition."

Out of My Deeper Heart

Out of my deeper heart a bird rose and flew skywards.

Higher and higher did it rise, yet larger and larger did it grow.

At first it was but like a swallow, then a lark, then an eagle, then as vast as a spring cloud, and then it filled the starry heavens.

Out of my heart a bird flew skywards. And it waxed larger as it flew. Yet it left not my heart.

O my faith, my untamed knowledge, how shall I fly to your height and see with you man's larger self penciled upon the sky?

How shall I turn this sea within me into mist, and move with you in space immeasurable?

How can a prisoner within the temple behold its golden domes?

How shall the heart of a fruit be stretched to envelop the fruit also?

O my faith, I am in chains behind these bars of silver and ebony, and I cannot fly with you.

Yet out of my heart you rise skyward, and it is my heart that holds you, and I shall be content.

Dynasties

The queen of Ishana was in travail of childbirth; and the king and the mighty men of his court were waiting in breathless anxiety in the great hall of the Winged Bulls.

At eventide there came suddenly a messenger in haste and prostrated himself before the king, and said, "I bring glad tidings unto my lord the king, and unto the kingdom and the slaves of the king. Mihrab the Cruel, thy life-long enemy, the king of Bethroun, is dead."

When the king and the mighty men heard this, they all rose and shouted for joy; for the powerful Mihrab, had he lived longer, had assuredly overcome Ishana and carried the inhabitants captive.

At this moment the court physician also entered the hall of Winged Bulls, and behind him came the royal midwives. And the physician prostrated himself before the king, and said, "My lord the king shall live for ever, and through countless generations shall he rule over the people of Ishana. For unto thee, O King, is born this very hour a son, who shall be thy heir."

Then indeed was the soul of the king intoxicated with joy, that in the same moment his foe was dead and the royal line was established.

Now in the city of Ishana lived a true prophet. And the prophet was young, and bold of spirit. And the king that very night ordered that the prophet should be brought before him. And when he was brought, the king said unto him, "Prophesy now, and foretell what shall be the future of my son who is this day born unto the kingdom."

And the prophet hesitated not, but said, "Hearken, O King, and I will indeed prophesy of the future of thy son that is this day born. The soul of thy enemy, even of thy enemy King Mihrab, who died yester-eve, lingered but a day upon the wind. Then it sought for itself a body to enter into. And that which it entered into was the body of thy son that is born unto thee this hour."

Then the king was enraged, and with his sword he slew the prophet.

And from that day to this, the wise men of Ishana say one to another secretly, "Is it not known, and has it not been said from of old, that Ishana is ruled by an enemy?"

Knowledge and Half-Knowledge

Four frogs sat upon a log that lay floating on the edge of a river. Suddenly the log was caught by the current and swept slowly down the stream. The frogs were delighted and absorbed, for never before had they sailed.

At length the first frog spoke, and said, "This is indeed a most marvelous log. It moves as if alive. No such log was ever known before."

Then the second frog spoke, and said, "Nay, my friend, the log is like other logs, and does not move. It is the river that is walking to the sea, and carries us and the log with it."

And the third frog spoke, and said, "It is neither the log nor the river that moves. The moving is in our thinking. For without thought nothing moves."

And the three frogs began to wrangle about what was really moving. The quarrel grew hotter and louder, but they could not agree.

Then they turned to the fourth frog, who up to this time had been listening attentively but holding his peace, and they asked his opinion.

And the fourth frog said, "Each of you is right, and none of you is wrong. The moving is in the log and the water and our thinking also."

And the three frogs became very angry, for none of them was willing to admit that his was not the whole truth, and that the other two were not wholly wrong.

Then a strange thing happened. The three frogs got together and pushed the fourth frog off the log into the river.

"Said A Sheet of Snow-White Paper . . ."

Said a sheet of snow-white paper, "Pure was I created, and pure will I remain for ever. I would rather be burnt and turn to white ashes than suffer darkness to touch me or the unclean to come near me."

The ink-bottle heard what the paper was saying, and it laughed in its dark heart; but it never dared to approach her. And the multicolored pencils heard her also, and they too never came near her.

And the snow-white sheet of paper did remain pure and chaste for ever, pure and chaste—and empty.

The Scholar And The Poet

Said the serpent to the lark, "Thou flyest, yet thou canst not visit the recesses of the earth where the sap of life moveth in perfect silence."

And the lark answered, "Aye, thou knowest over much, nay thou art wiser then all things wise—pity thou canst not fly."

And as if he did not hear, the serpent said, "Thou canst not see the secrets of the deep, nor move among the treasures of the hidden empire. It was but yesterday I lay in a cave of rubies. It is like the heart of a ripe pomegranate, and the faintest ray of light turns into a flame-rose. Who but me can behold such marvels?"

And the lark said, "None, none but thee can lie among the crystal memories of the cycles—pity thou canst not sing."

And the serpent said, "I know a plant whose root descends to the bowels of the earth, and he who eats of that root becomes fairer than Ashtarte."

And the lark said, "No one, no one but thee could inveil the magic thought of the earth—pity thou canst not fly."

And the serpent said, "There is a purple stream that runneth under a mountain, and he who drinketh of it shall become immortal even as the gods. Surely no bird or beast can discover that purple stream."

And the lark answered, "If thou willest thou canst become deathless even as the gods—pity thou canst not sing."

And the serpent said, "I know a buried temple, which I visit once a moon. It was built by a forgotten race of giants, and upon its walls are graven the secrets of time and space, and he who reads them shall understand that which passeth all understanding."

And the lark said, "Verily, if thou so desirest thou canst encircle with thy pliant body all knowledge of time and space—pity thou canst not fly."

Then the serpent was disgusted, and as he turned and entered into his hole he muttered, "Empty-headed songster!"

And the lark flew away singing, "Pity thou canst not sing. Pity, pity, my wise one, thou canst not fly."

Values

Once a man unearthed in his field a marble statue of great beauty. And he took it to a collector who loved all beautiful things and offered it to him for sale, and the collector bought it for a large price. And they parted.

And as the man walked home with his money he thought, and he said to himself, "How much life this money means! How can anyone give all this for a dead carved stone buried and undreamed of in the earth for a thousand years?"

And now the collector was looking at his statue, and he was thinking, and he said to himself, "What beauty! What life! The dream of what a soul! - and fresh with the sweet sleep of a thousand years. How can anyone give all this for money, dead and dreamless?"

Other Seas

A fish said to another fish, "Above this sea of ours there is another sea, with creatures swimming in it—and they live there even as we live here."

The fish replied, "Pure fancy! Pure fancy! When you know that everything that leaves our sea by even an inch, and stays out of it, dies. What proof have you of other lives in other seas?"

Repentance

On a moonless night a man entered into his neighbor's garden and stole the largest melon he could find and brought it home.

He opened it and found it still unripe.

Then behold a marvel!

The man's conscience woke and smote him with remorse; and he repented having stolen the melon.

The Dying Man and The Vulture

Wait, wait yet awhile, my eager friend.
I shall yield but too soon this wasted thing,
Whose agony overwrought and useless
Exhausts your patience.
I would not have your honest hunger
Wait upon these moments:
But this chain, though made of breath,
Is hard to break.
And the will to die,
Stronger than all things strong,
Is stayed by a will to live
Feebler than all things feeble.
Forgive me, comrade; I tarry too long.
It is memory that holds my spirit;
A procession of distant days,
A vision of youth spent in a dream,
A face that bids my eyelids not to sleep,
A voice that lingers in my ears,
A hand that touches my hand.
Forgive me that you have waited too long.
It is over now, and all is faded:
The face, the voice, the hand and the mist that
brought them hither.
The knot is untied.
The cord is cleaved.
And that which is neither food nor drink is
withdrawn.
Approach, my hungry comrade;
The board is made ready.
And the fare, frugal and spare,
Is given with love.
Come, and dig your beak here, into the left side,
And tear out of its cage this smaller bird,
Whose wings can beat no more:
I would have it soar with you into the sky.

Come now, my friend, I am your host tonight,
And you my welcome guest.

Beyond My Solitude

Beyond my solitude is another solitude, and to him who dwells therein my aloneness is a crowded market-place and my silence a confusion of sounds.

Too young am I and too restless to seek that above-solitude. The voices of yonder valley still hold my ears and its shadows bar my way and I cannot go.

Beyond these hills is a grove of enchantment and to him who dwells therein my peace is but a whirlwind and my enchantment an illusion.

Too young am I and too riotous to seek that sacred grove. The taste of blood is clinging in my mouth, and the bow and the arrows of my fathers yet linger in my hand and I cannot go.

Beyond this burdened self lives my freer self; and to him my dreams are a battle fought in twilight and my desires the rattling of bones.

Too young am I and too outraged to be my freer self.

And how shall I become my freer self unless I slay my burdened selves, or unless all men become free?

How shall the eagle in me soar against the sun until my fledglings leave the nest which I with my own beak have built for them?

The Last Watch

At high tide of night, when the first breath of dawn came upon the wind, the forerunner, he who calls himself echo to a voice yet unheard, left his bed-chamber and ascended to the roof of his house. Long he stood and looked down upon the slumbering city. Then he raised his head, and even as if the sleepless spirits of all those asleep had gathered around him, he opened his lips and spoke, and he said:

"My friends and neighbors and you who daily pass my gate, I would speak to you in your sleep, and in the valley of your dreams I would walk naked and unrestrained; for heedless are your waking hours and deaf are your sound-burdened ears.

"Long did I love you and overmuch.

"I love the one among you as though he were all, and all as if you were one. And in the spring of my heart I sang in your gardens, and in the summer of my heart I watched at your threshing-floors.

"Yea, I loved you all, the giant and the pygmy, the leper and the anointed, and him who gropes in the dark even as him who dances his days upon the mountains.

"You, the strong, have I loved, though the marks of your iron hoofs are yet upon my flesh; and you the weak, though you have drained my faith and wasted my patience.

"You the rich have I loved, while bitter was your honey to my mouth; and you the poor, though you knew my empty-handed shame.

"You the poet with the bowed lute and blind fingers, you have I loved in self-indulgence; and you the scholar ever gathering rotted shrouds in potters' fields.

"You the priest I have loved, who sit in the silences of yesterday questioning the fate of my tomorrow; and you the worshippers of gods the images of your own desires.

"You the thirsting woman whose cup is ever full, I have loved in understanding; and you the woman of restless nights, you too I have loved in pity.

"You the talkative have I loved, saying, 'Life hath much to say'; and you the dumb have I loved, whispering to myself, 'Says he not in silence that which I fain would hear in words?'

"And you the judge and the critic, I have loved also; yet when you have seen me crucified, you said, 'He bleeds rhythmically, and the pattern his blood makes upon his white skin is beautiful to behold.'

"Yea, I have loved you all, the young and the old, the trembling reed and the oak.

"But, alas, it was the over-abundance of my heart that turned you from me. You would drink love from a cup, but not from a surging river. You would hear love's faint murmur, but when love shouts you would muffle your ears.

"And because I have loved you all you have said, 'Too soft and yielding is his heart, and too undiscerning is his path. It is the love of a needy one, who picks crumbs even as he sits at kingly feasts. And it is the love of a weakling, for the strong loves only the strong."

"And because I have loved you overmuch you have said, 'It is but the love of a blind man who knows not the beauty of one nor the ugliness of another. And it is the love of the tasteless who drinks vinegar even as wine. And it is the love of the impertinent and the overweening, for what stranger could be our mother and father and sister and brother?'

"This you have said, and more. For often in the market-place you pointed your fingers at me and said mockingly, 'There goes the ageless one, the man without seasons, who at the noon hour plays games with our children and at eventide sits with our elders and assumes wisdom and understanding.'

"And I said, 'I will love them more. Aye, even more. I will hide my love with seeming to hate, and disguise my tenderness as bitterness. I will wear an iron mask, and only when armed and mailed shall I seek them.'

"Then I laid a heavy hand upon your bruises, and like a tempest in the night I thundered in your ears.

"From the housetop I proclaimed you hypocrites, Pharisees, tricksters, false and empty earth-bubbles.

"The short-sighted among you I cursed for blind bats, and those too near the earth I likened to soulless moles.

"The eloquent I pronounced fork-tongued, the silent, stone-lipped, and the simple and artless I called the dead never weary of death.

"The seekers after world knowledge I condemned as offenders of the holy spirit and those who would naught but the spirit I branded as hunters of shadows who cast their nets in flat waters and catch but their own images.

"Thus with my lips have I denounced you, while my heart, bleeding within me, called you tender names.

"It was love lashed by its own self that spoke. It was pride half slain that fluttered in the dust. It was my hunger for your love that raged from the housetop, while my own love, kneeling in silence, prayed your forgiveness.

"But behold a miracle!

"It was my disguise that opened your eyes, and my seeming to hate that woke your hearts.

"And now you love me.

"You love the swords that stroke you and the arrows that crave your breast. For it comforts you to be wounded and only when you drink of your own blood can you be intoxicated.

"Like moths that seek destruction in the flame you gather daily in my garden; and with faces uplifted and eyes enchanted you watch me tear the fabric of your days. And in whispers you say the one to the other, 'He sees with the light of God. He speaks like the prophets of old. He unveils our souls and unlocks our hearts, and like the eagle that knows the way of foxes he knows our ways.'

"Aye, in truth, I know your ways, but only as an eagle knows the ways of his fledglings. And I fain would disclose my secret. Yet in my need for your nearness I feign remoteness, and in fear of the ebb tide of your love I guard the floodgates of my love."

After saying these things the forerunner covered his face with his hands and wept bitterly. For he knew in his heart that love humiliated in its nakedness is greater than love that seeks triumph in disguise; and he was ashamed.

But suddenly he raised his head, and like one waking from sleep he outstretched his arms and said, "Night is over, and we children of night must die when dawn comes leaping upon the hills; and out of our ashes a mightier love shall rise. And it shall laugh in the sun, and it shall be deathless.

The Wanderer

1932 (posthumously)

The Wanderer

I met him at the crossroads, a man with but a cloak and a staff, and a veil of pain upon his face. And we greeted one another, and I said to him, "Come to my house and be my guest."

And he came.

My wife and my children met us at the threshold, and he smiled at them, and they loved his coming.

Then we all sat together at the board and we were happy with the man for there was a silence and a mystery in him.

And after supper we gathered to the fire and I asked him about his wanderings.

He told us many a tale that night and also the next day, but what I now record was born out of the bitterness of his days though he himself was kindly, and these tales are of the dust and patience of his road.

And when he left us after three days we did not feel that a guest had departed but rather that one of us was still out in the garden and had not yet come in.

Garments

Upon a day Beauty and Ugliness met on the shore of a sea. And they said to one another, "Let us bathe in the sea."

Then they disrobed and swam in the waters. And after a while Ugliness came back to shore and garmented himself with the garments of Beauty and walked away.

And Beauty too came out of the sea, and found not her raiment, and she was too shy to be naked, therefore she dressed herself with the raiment of Ugliness. And Beauty walked her way.

And to this very day men and women mistake the one for the other.

Yet some there are who have beheld the face of Beauty, and they know her notwithstanding her garments. And some there be who know the face of Ugliness, and the cloth conceals him not from their eyes.

The Eagle and the Skylark

A skylark and an eagle met on a rock upon a high hill. The skylark said, "Good morrow to you, Sir." And the eagle looked down upon him and said faintly, "Good morrow."

And the skylark said, "I hope all things are well with you, Sir."

"Aye," said the eagle, "all is well with us. But do you not know that we are the king of birds, and that you shall not address us before we ourselves have spoken?"

Said the skylark, "Methinks we are of the same family."

The eagle looked upon him with disdain and he said, "Who ever has said that you and I are of the same family?"

Then said the skylark, "But I would remind you of this, I can fly even as high as you, and I can sing and give delight to the other creatures of this earth. And you give neither pleasure nor delight."

Then the eagle was angered, and he said, "Pleasure and delight! You little presumptuous creature! With one thrust of my beak I could destroy you. You are but the size of my foot."

Then the skylark flew up and alighted upon the back of the eagle and began to pick at his feathers. The eagle was annoyed, and he flew swift and high that he might rid himself of the little bird. But he failed to do so. At last he dropped back to that very rock upon the high hill, more fretted than ever, with the little creature still upon his back, and cursing the fate of the hour.

Now at that moment a small turtle came by and laughed at the sight, and laughed so hard the she almost turned upon her back.

And the eagle looked down upon the turtle and he said, "You slow creeping thing, ever one with the earth, what are you laughing at?"

And the turtle said, "Why I see that you are turned horse, and that you have a small bird riding you, but the small bird is the better bird."

And the eagle said to her, "Go you about your business. This is a family affair between my brother, the lark, and myself."

The Love Song

A poet once wrote a love song and it was beautiful. And he made many copies of it, and sent them to his friends and his acquaintances, both men and women, and even to a young woman whom he had met but once, who lived beyond the mountains.

And in a day or two a messenger came from the young woman bringing a letter. And in the letter she said, "Let me assure you, I am deeply touched by the love song that you have written to me. Come now, and see my father and my mother, and we shall make arrangements for the betrothal."

And the poet answered the letter, and he said to her, "My friend, it was but a song of love out of a poet's heart, sung by every man to every woman."

And she wrote again to him saying, "Hypocrite and liar in words! From this day unto my coffin-day I shall hate all poets for your sake."

Tears and Laughter

Upon the bank of the Nile at eventide, a hyena met a crocodile and they stopped and greeted one another.

The hyena spoke and said, "How goes the day with you, Sir?"

And the crocodile answered saying, "It goes badly with me. Sometimes in my pain and sorrow I weep, and then the creatures always say, 'They are but crocodile tears.' And this wounds me beyond all telling."

Then the hyena said, "You speak of your pain and your sorrow, but think of me also, for a moment. I gaze at the beauty of the world, its wonders and its miracles, and out of sheer joy I laugh even as the day laughs. And then the people of the jungle say, 'It is but the laughter of a hyena.'"

At the Fair

There came to the Fair a girl from the country-side, most comely. There was a lily and a rose in her face.

There was a sunset in her hair, and dawn smiled upon her lips.

No sooner did the lovely stranger appear in their sight than the young men sought her and surrounded her. One would dance with her, and another would cut a cake in her honor. And they all desired to kiss her cheek. For after all, was it not the Fair?

But the girl was shocked and started, and she thought ill of the young men. She rebuked them, and she even struck one or two of them in the face. Then she ran away from them.

And on her way home that evening she was saying in her heart, "I am disgusted. How unmannerly and ill bred are these men. It is beyond all patience."

A year passed during which that very comely girl thought much of Fairs and men. Then she came again to the Fair with the lily and the rose in her face, the sunset in her hair and the smile of dawn upon her lips.

But now the young men, seeing her, turned from her. And all the day long she was unsought and alone.

And at eventide as she walked the road toward her home she cried in her heart, "I am disgusted. How unmannerly and ill bred are these youths. It is beyond all patience."

The Two Princesses

In the city of Shawakis lived a prince, and he was loved by everyone, men and women and children. Even the animals of the field came unto him in greeting.

But all the people said that his wife, the princess, loved him not; nay, that she even hated him.

And upon a day the princess of a neighboring city came to visit the princess of Shawakis. And they sat and talked together, and their words led to their husbands.

And the princess of Sharakis said with passion, "I envy you your happiness with the prince, your husband, though you have been married these many years. I hate my husband. He belongs not to me alone, and I am indeed a woman most unhappy."

Then the visiting princess gazed at her and said, "My friend, the truth is that you love your husband. Aye, and you still have him for a passion unspent, and that is life in woman like unto Spring in a garden. But pity me, and my husband, for we do but endure one another in silent patience. And yet you and others deem this happiness."

The Lightning Flash

There was a Christian bishop in his cathedral on a stormy day, and an un-Christian woman came and stood before him, and she said, "I am not a Christian. Is there salvation for me from hell-fire?"

And the bishop looked upon the woman, and he answered her saying, "Nay, there is salvation for those only who are baptized of water and of the spirit."

And even as he spoke a bolt from the sky fell with thunder upon the cathedral and it was filled with fire.

And the men of the city came running, and they saved the woman, but the bishop was consumed, food of the fire.

The Hermit and the Beasts

Once there lived among the green hills a hermit. He was pure of spirit and white of heart. And all the animals of the land and all the fowls of the air came to him in pairs and he spoke unto them. They heard him gladly, and they would gather near unto him, and would not go until nightfall, when he would send them away, entrusting them to the wind and the woods with his blessing.

Upon an evening as he was speaking of love, a leopard raised her head and said to the hermit, "You speak to us of loving. Tell us, Sir, where is your mate?"

And the hermit said, "I have no mate."

Then a great cry of surprise rose from the company of beasts and fowls, and they began to say among themselves, "How can he tell us of loving and mating when he himself knows naught thereof?" And quietly and in distain they left him alone.

That night the hermit lay upon his mat with his face earthward, and he wept bitterly and beat his hands upon his breast.

The Prophet and the Child

Once on a day the prophet Sharia met a child in a garden. The child ran to him and said, "Good morrow to you, Sir," and the prophet said, "Good morrow to you, Sir." And in a moment, "I see that you are alone."

Then the child said, in laughter and delight, "It took a long time to lose my nurse. She thinks I am behind those hedges; but can't you see that I am here?" Then he gazed at the prophet's face and spoke again. "You are alone, too. What did you do with your nurse?"

The prophet answered and said, "Ah, that is a different thing. In very truth I cannot lose her oftentime. But now, when I came into this garden, she was seeking after me behind the hedges."

The child clapped his hands and cried out, "So you are like me! Isn't it good to be lost?" And then he said, "Who are you?"

And the man answered, "They call me the prophet Sharia. And tell me, who are you?"

"I am only myself," said the child, "and my nurse is seeking after me, and she does not know where I am."

Then the prophet gazed into space saying, "I too have escaped my nurse for awhile, but she will find me out."

And the child said, "I know mine will find me out too."

At that moment a woman's voice was heard calling the child's name. "See," said the child, "I told you she would be finding me."

And at the same moment another voice was heard, "Where art thou, Sharia?"

And the prophet said, "See my child, they have found me also."

And turning his face upward, Sharia answered, "Here I am."

The Pearl

Said one oyster to a neighboring oyster, "I have a very great pain within me. It is heavy and round and I am in distress."

And the other oyster replied with haughty complacence, "Praise be to the heavens and to the sea, I have no pain within me. I am well and whole both within and without."

At that moment a crab was passing by and heard the two oysters, and he said to the one who was well and whole both within and without, "Yes, you are well and whole; but the pain that your neighbor bears is a pearl of exceeding beauty."

Body and Soul

A man and a woman sat by a window that opened upon Spring. They sat close one unto the other. And the woman said, "I love you. You are handsome, and you are rich, and you are always well-attired."

And the man said, "I love you. You are a beautiful thought, a thing too apart to hold in the hand, and a song in my dreaming."

But the woman turned from him in anger, and she said, "Sir, please leave me now. I am not a thought, and I am not a thing that passes in your dreams. I am a woman. I would have you desire me, a wife, and the mother of unborn children."

And they parted.

And the man was saying in his heart, "Behold another dream is even now turned into mist."

And the woman was saying, "Well, what of a man who turns me into a mist and a dream?"

The King

The people of the kingdom of Sadik surrounded the palace of their king shouting in rebellion against him. And he came down the steps of the palace carrying his crown in one hand and his scepter in the other. The majesty of his appearance silenced the multitude, and he stood before them and said, "My friends, who are no longer my subjects, here I yield my crown and scepter unto you. I would be one of you. I am only one man, but as a man I would work together with you that our lot may be made better. There is no need for king. Let us go therefore to the fields and the vineyards and labor hand with hand. Only you must tell me to what field or vineyard I should go. All of you now are king."

And the people marveled, and stillness was upon them, for the king whom they had deemed the source of their discontent now yielding his crown and scepter to them and became as one of them.

Then each and every one of them went his way, and the king walked with one man to a field.

But the Kingdom of Sadik fared not better without a king, and the mist of discontent was still upon the land. The people cried out in the market places saying that they have a king to rule them. And the elders and the youths said as if with one voice, "We will have our king."

And they sought the king and found him toiling in the field, and they brought him to his seat, and yielded unto his crown and his scepter. And they said, "Now rule us, with might and with justice."

And he said, "I will indeed rule you with might, and may the gods of the heaven and the earth help me that I may also rule with justice."

Now, there came to his presence men and women and spoke unto him of a baron who mistreated them, and to whom they were but serfs.

And straightway the king brought the baron before him and said, "The life of one man is as weighty in the scales of God as the life of another. And because you know not how to weigh the lives of those who work in your fiends and your vineyards, you are banished, and you shall leave this kingdom forever."

The following day came another company to the king and spoke of the cruelty of a countess beyond the hills, and how she brought them down to misery. Instantly the countess was brought to court, and the king sentenced her also to banishment, saying, "Those who till our fields and care for our vineyards are nobler than we who eat the bread they prepare and drink the wine of their wine-press. And because you know not this, you shall leave this land and be afar from this kingdom."

Then came men and women who said that the bishop made them bring stones and hew the stones for the cathedral, yet he gave them naught, though they knew the bishop's coffer was full of gold and silver while they themselves were empty with hunger.

And the king called for the bishop, and when the bishop came the king spoke and said unto his, "That cross you wear upon your bosom should mean giving life unto life. But you have taken life from life and you have given none. Therefore you shall leave this kingdom never to return."

Thus each day for a full moon men and women came to the king to tell him of the burdens laid upon them. And each and every day a full moon some oppressor was exiled from the land.

And the people of Sadik were amazed, and there was cheer in their heart.

And upon a day the elders and the youths came and surrounded the tower of the king and called for him. And he came down holding his crown with one hand and his scepter with the other.

And he spoke unto and said, "Now, what would you do of me? Behold, I yield back to you that which you desired me to hold."

But they cried. "Nay, nay, you are our rightful king. You have made clean the land of vipers, and you have brought the wolves to naught, and we welcome to sing our thanksgiving unto you. The crown is yours in majesty and the scepter is yours in glory."

Then the king said, "Not I, not I. You yourselves are king. When you deemed me weak and a misruler, you yourselves were weak and misruling. And now the land fares well because it is in your will. I am but a thought in the mind of you all, and I exist not save in your actions. There is no such person as governor. Only the governed exist to govern themselves."

And the king re-entered his tower with his crown and his scepter. And the elders and the youths went their various ways and they were content.

And each and every one thought of himself as king with a crown in one hand and a scepter in the other.

Upon the Sand

Said one man to another, "At the high tide of the sea, long ago, with the point of my staff I wrote a line upon the sand; and the people still pause to read it, and they are careful that naught shall erase it."

And the other man said, "And I to wrote a line upon the sand, but it was at low tide, and the waves of the vast sea washed it away. But tell me, what did you write?"

And the first man answered and said, "I wrote this: 'I am he who is.' But what did you write?"

And the other man said, "This I wrote: 'I am but a drop of this great ocean.'"

The Three Gifts

Once in the city of Becharre there lived a gracious prince who was loved and honored by all his subjects.

But there was one exceedingly poor man who was bitter against the prince, and who wagged continually a pestilent tongue in his dispraise.

The prince knew this, yet he was patient.

But at last he bethought him; and upon a wintry night there came to the door of the man a servant of the prince, bearing a sack of flour, a bag of soap and a cone of sugar.

And the servant said, "The prince sends you these gifts in token of remembrance."

The man was elated, for he thought the gifts were an homage from the prince. And in his pride we went to the bishop and told him what the prince had done, saying, "Can you not see how the prince desires my goodwill?"

But the bishop said, "Oh, how wise a prince, and how little you understand. He speaks in symbols. The flour is for your empty stomach; the soap is for your dirty hide; and the sugar is to sweeten your bitter tongue."

From that day forward the man became shy even of himself. His hatred of the prince was greater than ever, and even more he hated the bishop who had revealed the prince unto him.

But thereafter he kept silent.

Peace and War

Three dogs were basking in the sun and conversing. The first dog said dreamily, "It is indeed wondrous to be living in this day of dogdom. Consider the ease with which we travel under the sea, upon the earth and even in the sky. And meditate for a moment upon the inventions brought forth for the comfort of dogs, even for our eyes and ears and noses."

And the second dog spoke and he said, "We are more heedful of the arts. We bark at the moon more rhythmically than did our forefathers. And when we gaze at ourselves in the water we see that our features are clearer than the features of yesterday."

Then the third dog spoke and said, "But what interests me most and beguiles my mind is the tranquil understanding existing between dogdoms."

At that very moment they looked, and lo, the dog-catcher was approaching.

The three dogs sprang up and scampered down the street; and as they ran the third dog said, "For God's sake, run for your lives. Civilization is after us."

The Dancer

Once there came to the court of the Prince of Birkasha a dancer with her musicians. And she was admitted to the court, and she danced before the prince to the music the lute and the flute and the zither.

She danced the dance of flames, and the dance of swords and spears; she danced the dance of stars and the dance of space. And then she danced the dance of flowers in the wind.

After this she stood before the throne of the prince and bowed her body before him. And the prince bade her to come nearer, and he said unto her, "Beautiful woman, daughter of grace and delight, whence comes your art? And how is it that you command all the elements in your rhythms and your rhymes?"

And the dancer bowed again before the prince, and she answered, "Mighty and gracious Majesty, I know not the answer to your questionings. Only this I know: The philosopher's soul dwells in his head, the poet's soul is in the heart; the singer's soul lingers about his throat, but the soul of the dancer abides in all her body."

The Two Guardian Angels

On an evening two angels met at the city gate, and they greeted one another, and they conversed.

The one angel said, "What are you doing these days, and what work is given you?"

And the other answered, "It was been assigned me to be the guardian of a fallen man who lives down in the valley, a great sinner, most degraded. Let me assure you it is an important task, and I work hard."

The first fallen angel said, "That is an easy commission. I have often known sinners, and have been their guardian many a time. But it has now been assigned me to be the guardian of the good saint who lives in a bower out yonder. And I assure you that is an exceedingly difficult work, and most subtle."

Said the first angel, "This is but assumption. How can guarding a saint be harder than guarding a sinner?"

And the other answered, "What impertinence, to call me assumptious! I have stated but the truth. Methinks it is you who are assumptious!"

Then the angels wrangled and fought, first with words and then with fists and wings.

While they were fighting an archangel came by. And he stopped them, and said, "Why do you fight? And what is it all about? Know you not that it is most unbecoming for guardian angels to fight at the city gate? Tell me, what is your disagreement?"

Then both angels spoke at once, each claiming that the work given him was the harder, and that he deserved the greater recognition.

The archangel shook his head and bethought him.

Then he said, "My friends, I cannot say now which one of you has the greater claim upon honor and reward. But since the power is bestowed in me, therefore for peace' sake and for good guardianship, I give each of you the other's occupation, since each of you insists that the other's task is the easier one. Now go hence and be happy at your work."

The angels thus ordered went their ways. But each one looked backward with greater anger at the archangel. And in his heart each was saying, "Oh, these archangels! Every day they make life harder and still harder for us angels!"

But the archangel stood there, and once more he bethought him. And he said in his heart, "We have indeed, to be watchful and to keep guard over our guardian angels."

The Statue

Once there lived a man among the hills who possessed a statue wrought by an ancient master. It lay at his door face downward and he was not mindful of it.

One day there passed by his house a man from the city, a man of knowledge, and seeing the statue he inquired of the owner if he would sell it.

The owner laughed and said, "And pray who would want to buy that dull and dirty stone?"

The man from the city said, "I will give you this piece of silver for it."

And the other man was astonished and delighted.

The statue was removed to the city, upon the back of and elephant. And after many moons the man from the hills visited the city, and as he walked the streets he saw a crowd before a shop, and a man with a loud voice was crying, "Come ye in and behold the most beautiful, the most wonderful statue in all the world. Only two silver pieces to look upon this most marvelous work of a master."

Thereupon the man from the hills paid two silver pieces and entered the shop to see the statue that he himself had sold for one piece of silver.

The Exchange

Once upon a crossroad a poor Poet met a rich Stupid, and they conversed. And all that they said revealed but their discontent.

Then the Angel of the Road passed by, and he laid his hand upon the shoulder of the two men.

And behold, a miracle: The two men had now exchanged their possessions.

And they parted. But strange to relate, the Poet looked and found naught in his hand but dry moving sand; and the Stupid closed his eyes and felt naught but moving cloud in his heart.

Love and Hate

A woman said unto a man, "I love you." And the man said, "It is in my heart to be worthy of your love."

Ant he woman said, "You love me not?"

And the man only gazed upon her and said nothing.

Then the woman cried aloud, "I hate you."

And the man said, "Then it is also in my heart to be worthy of your hate."

Dreams

A man dreamed a dream, and when he awoke he went to his soothsayer and desired that his dream be made plain unto him.

And the soothsayer said to the man, "Come to me with the dreams that you behold in your wakefulness and I will tell you their meaning. But the dreams of your sleep belong neither to my wisdom nor to your imagination."

The Madman

It was in the garden of a madhouse that I met a youth with a face pale and lovely and full of wonder. And I sat beside him upon the bench, and I said, "Why are you here?"

And he looked at me in astonishment, and he said, "It is an unseemly question, yet I will answer you. My father would make of me a reproduction of himself; so also would my uncle. My mother would have me the image of her seafaring husband as the perfect example for me to follow. My brother thinks I should be like him, a fine athlete.

"And my teachers also, the doctor of philosophy, and the music-master, and the logician, they too were determined, and each would have me but a reflection of his own face in a mirror.

"Therefore I came to this place. I find it more sane here. At least, I can be myself."

Then of a sudden he turned to me and he said, "But tell me, were you also driven to this place by education and good counsel?"

And I answered, "No, I am a visitor."

And he answered, "Oh, you are one of those who live in the madhouse on the other side of the wall."

The Frogs

Upon a summer day a frog said to his mate, "I fear those people living in that house on the shore are disturbed by our night-songs."

And his mate answered and said, "Well, do they not annoy our silence during the day with their talking?"

The frog said, "Let us not forget that we may sing too much in the night."

And his mate answered, "Let us not forget that they chatter and shout overmuch during the day."

Said the frog, "How about the bullfrog who that they clatter and shout overmuch during the day."

Said the frog, "How about the bullfrog who disturbs the whole neighborhood with his God-forbidden booming?"

And his mate replied, "Aye, and what say you of the politician and the priest and the scientist who come to these shores and fill the air with noisy and rhymeless sound?"

Then the frog said, "Well, let us be better than these human beings. Let us be quiet at night, and keep our songs in our hearts, even though the moon calls for our rhythm and the stars for our rhyme. At least, let us be silent for a night or two, or even for three nights."

And his mate said, "Very well, I agree. We shall see what your bountiful heart will bring forth."

That night the frogs were silent; and they were silent the following night also, and again upon the third night.

And strange to relate, the talkative woman who lived in the house beside the lake came down to breakfast on that third day and shouted to her husband, "I have not slept these three nights. I was secure with sleep when the noise of the frogs was in my ear. But something must have happened. They have not sung now for three nights; and I am almost maddened with sleeplessness."

The frog heard this and turned to his mate and said, winking his eye, "And we were almost maddened with our silence, were we not?"

And his mate answered, "Yes, the silence of the night was heavy upon us. And I can see now that there is no need for us to cease our singing for the comfort of those who must needs fill their emptiness with noise."

And that night the moon called not in vain for their rhythm nor the stars for their rhyme.

Laws and Law-Giving

Ages ago there was a great king, and he was wise. And he desired to lay laws unto his subjects.

He called upon one thousand wise men of one thousand different tribes to his capitol and lay down the laws.

And all this came to pass.

But when the thousand laws written upon parchment were put before the king and he read them, he wept bitterly in his soul, for he had not known that there were one thousand forms of crime in his kingdom.

Then he called his scribe, and with a smile upon his mouth he himself dictated laws. And his laws were but seven.

And the one thousand wise men left him in anger and returned to their tribes with the laws they had laid down. And every tribe followed the laws of its wise men.

Therefore they have a thousand laws even to our own day.

It is a great country, but it has one thousand prisons, and the prisons are full of women and men, breakers of a thousand laws.

It is indeed a great country, but the people thereof are descendants of one thousand law-givers and of only one wise king.

Yesterday, Today and Tomorrow

I said to my friend, "You see her leaning upon the arm of that man. It was but yesterday that she leaned thus upon my arm."

And my friend said, "And tomorrow she will lean upon mine."

I said, "Behold her sitting close at his side. It was but yesterday she sat close beside me."

And he answered, "Tomorrow she will sit beside me."

I said, "See, she drinks wine from his cup, and yesterday she drank from mine."

And he said, "Tomorrow, from my cup."

Then I said, "See how she gazes at him with love, and with yielding eyes. Yesterday she gazed thus upon me."

And my friend said, "It will be upon me she gazes tomorrow."

I said, "Do you not hear her now murmuring songs of love into his ears? Those very songs of love she murmured but yesterday into my ears."

And my friend said, "And tomorrow she will murmur them in mine."

I said, "Why see, she is embracing him. It was but yesterday that she embraced me."

And my friend said, "She will embrace me tomorrow."

Then I said, "What a strange woman."

But he answered, "She is like unto life, possessed by all men; and like death, she conquers all men; and like eternity, she enfolds all men."

The Philosopher and the Cobbler

There came to a cobbler's shop a philosopher with worn shoes. And the philosopher said to the cobbler, "Please mend my shoes."

And the cobbler said, "I am mending another man's shoes now, and there are still other shoes to patch before I can come to yours. But leave your shoes here, and wear this other pair today, and come tomorrow for your own."

Then the philosopher was indignant, and he said, "I wear no shoes that are not mine own."

And the cobbler said, "Well then, are you in truth a philosopher, and cannot enfold your feet with the shoes of another man? Upon this very street there is another cobbler who understands philosophers better than I do. Go you to him for mending."

Builders of Bridges

In Antioch where the river Assi goes to meet the sea, a bridge was built to bring one half of the city nearer to the other half. It was built of large stones carried down from among the hills, on the backs of the mules of Antioch.

When the bridge was finished, upon a pillar thereof was engraved in Greek and in Aramaic, "This bridge was built by King Antiochus II."

And all the people walked across the good bridge over the goodly river Assi.

And upon an evening, a youth, deemed by some a little mad, descended to the pillar where the words were engraven, and he covered over the graving with charcoal, and above it wrote, "The stones of this bridge were brought down from the hills by the mules. In passing to and fro over it you are riding upon the backs of the mules of Antioch, builders of this bridge."

And when the people read what the youth had written, some of them laughed and some marveled. And some said, "Ah yes, we know who has done this. Is he not a little mad?"

But one mule said, laughing, to another mule, "Do you not remember that we did carry those stones? And yet until now it has been said that the bridge was built by King Antiochus."

The Field of Zaad

Upon the road of Zaad a traveler met a man who lived in a nearby village, and the traveler, pointing with his hand to a vast field, asked the man saying, "Was not this the battle-ground where King Ahlam overcame his enemies?"

And the man answered and said, "This has never been a battle-ground. There once stood on this field the great city of Zaad, and it was burnt down to ashes. But now it is a good field, is it not?"

And the traveler and the man parted.

Not a half mile farther the traveler met another man, and pointing to the field again, he said, "So that is where the great city of Zaad once stood?'

And the man said, "There has never been a city in this place. But once there was a monastery here, and it was destroyed by the people of the South Country."

Shortly after, on that very road of Zaad, the traveler met a third man, and pointing once more to the vast field he said, "Is it not true that this is the place where once there stood a great monastery?"

But the man answered, "There has never been a monastery in this neighborhood, but our fathers and our forefathers have told us that once there fell a great meteor on this field."

Then the traveler walked on, wondering in his heart. And he met a very old man, and saluting his he said, "Sir, upon this road I have met three men who live in the neighborhood and I have asked each of them about this field, and each one denied what the other had said, and each one told me a new tale that the other had not told."

Then the old man raised his head, and answered, "My friend, each and every one of these men told you what was indeed so; but few of us are able to add fact to different fact and make a truth thereof."

The Golden Belt

Once upon a day two men who met on the road were walking together toward Salamis, the City of Columns. In the mid-afternoon they came to a wide river and there was no bridge to cross it. They must needs swim, or seek another road unknown to them.

And they said to one another, "Let us swim. After all, the river is not so wide." And they threw themselves into the water and swam.

And one of the men who had always known rivers and the ways of rivers, in mid-stream suddenly began to lose himself; and to be carried away by the rushing waters; while the other who had never swum before crossed the river straight-way and stood upon the farther bank. Then seeing his companion still wrestling with the stream, he threw himself again into the waters and brought him also safely to the shore.

And the man who had been swept away by the current said, "But you told me you could not swim. How then did you cross that river with such assurance?"

And the second man answered, "My friend, do you see this belt which girdles me? It is full of golden coins that I have earned for my wife and my children, a full year's work. It is the weight of this belt of gold that carried me across the river, to my wife and my children. And my wife and my children were upon my shoulders as I swam."

And the two men walked on together toward Salamis.

The Red Earth

Said a tree to a man, "My roots are in the deep red earth, and I shall give you of my fruit."

And the man said to the tree, "How alike we are. My roots are also deep in the red earth. And the red earth gives you power to bestow upon me of your fruit, and the red earth teaches me to receive from you with thanksgiving."

The Full Moon

The full moon rose in glory upon the town, and all the dogs of that town began to bark at the moon.

Only one dog did not bark, and he said to them in a grave voice, "Awake not stillness from her sleep, nor bring you the moon to the earth with your barking."

Then all the dogs ceased barking, in awful silence. But the dog who had spoken to them continued barking for silence, the rest of the night.

The Hermit Prophet

Once there lived a hermit prophet, and thrice a moon he would go down to the great city and in the market places he would preach giving and sharing to the people. And he was eloquent, and his fame was upon the land.

Upon an evening three men came to his hermitage and he greeted them. And they said, "You have been preaching giving and sharing, and you have sought to teach those who have much to give unto those who have little; and we doubt not that your fame has brought you riches. Now come and give us of your riches, for we are in need."

And the hermit answered and said, "My friends, I have naught but this bed and this mat and this jug of water. Take them if it is in your desire. I have neither gold nor silver."

Then they looked down with distain upon him, and turned their faces from him, and the last man stood at the door for a moment, and said, "Oh, you cheat! You fraud! You teach and preach that which you yourself do not perform."

The Old, Old Wine

Once there lived a rich man who was justly proud of his cellar and the wine therein. And there was one jug of ancient vintage kept for some occasion known only to himself.

The governor of the state visited him, and he bethought him and said, "That jug shall not be opened for a mere governor."

And a bishop of the diocese visited him, but he said to himself, "Nay, I will not open that jug. He would not know its value, nor would its aroma reach his nostrils."

The prince of the realm came and supped with him. But he thought, "It is too royal a wine for a mere princeling."

And even on the day when his own nephew was married, he said to himself, "No, not to these guests shall that jug be brought forth."

And the years passed by, and he died, an old man, and he was buried like unto every seed and acorn.

And upon the day that he was buried the ancient jug was brought out together with other jugs of wine, and it was shared by the peasants of the neighborhood. And none knew its great age.

To them, all that is poured into a cup is only wine.

The Two Poems

Many centuries ago, on a road to Athens, two poets met, and they were glad to see one another.

And one poet asked the other saying, "What have you composed of late, and how goes it with your lyre?"

And the other poet answered and said with pride, "I have but now finished the greatest of my poems, perchance the greatest poem yet written in Greek. It is an invocation to Zeus the Supreme."

Then he took from beneath his cloak a parchment, saying, "Here, behold, I have it with me, and I would fain read it to you. Come, let us sit in the shade of that white cypress."

And the poet read his poem. And it was a long poem.

And the other poet said in kindliness, "This is a great poem. It will live through the ages, and in it you shall be glorified."

And the first poet said calmly, "And what have you been writing these late days?"

And the other another, "I have written but little. Only eight lines in remembrance of a child playing in a garden." And he recited the lines.

The first poet said, "Not so bad; not so bad."

And they parted.

And now after two thousand years the eight lines of the one poet are read in every tongue, and are loved and cherished.

And though the other poem has indeed come down through the ages in libraries and in the cells of scholars, and though it is remembered, it is neither loved nor read.

Lady Ruth

Three men once looked from afar upon a white house that stood alone on a green hill. One of them said, "That is the house of Lady Ruth. She is an old witch."

The second man said, "You are wrong. Lady Ruth is a beautiful woman who lives there consecrated unto her dreams."

The third man said, "You are both wrong. Lady Ruth is the holder of this vast land, and she draws blood from her serfs."

And they walked on discussing Lady Ruth. Then when they came to a crossroad they met an old man, and one of them asked him, saying, "Would you please tell us about the Lady Ruth who lives in that white house upon the hill?"

And the old man raised his head and smiled upon them, and said, "I am ninety of years, and I remember Lady Ruth when I was but a boy. But Lady Ruth died eighty years ago, and now the house is empty. The owls hoot therein, sometimes, and people say the place is haunted."

The Mouse and the Cat

Once on an evening a poet met a peasant. The poet was distant and the peasant was shy, yet they conversed.

And the peasant said, "Let me tell you a little story which I heard of late. A mouse was caught in a trap, and while he was happily eating the cheese that lay therein, a cat stood by. The mouse trembled awhile, but he knew he was safe within the trap.

"Then the cat said, 'You are eating your last meal, my friend.'

"'Yes,' answered the mouse, 'one life have I, therefore one death. But what of you? They tell me you have nine lives. Doesn't that mean that you will have to die nine times?'"

And the peasant looked at the poet and he said, "Is not this a strange story?"

And the poet answered him not, but he walked away saying in his soul, "To be sure, nine lives have we, nine lives to be sure. And we shall die nine times, nine times shall we die. Perhaps it were better to have but one life, caught in a trap — the life of a peasant with a bit of cheese for the last meal. And yet, are we not kin unto the lions of the desert and the jungle?"

The Curse

And old man of the sea once said to me, "It was thirty years ago that a sailor ran away with my daughter. And I cursed them both in my heart, for of all the world I loved but my daughter.

"Not long after that, the sailor youth went down with his ship to the bottom of the sea, and with him my lovely daughter was lost unto me.

"Now therefore behold in me the murderer of a youth and a maid. It was my curse that destroyed them. And now on my way to the grave I seek God's forgiveness."

This the old man said. But there was a tone of bragging in his words, and it seems that he is still proud of the power of his curse.

The Shadow

Upon a June day the grass said to the shadow of an elm tree, "You move to right and left over-often, and you disturb my peace."

And the shadow answered and said, "Not I, not I. Look skyward. There is a tree that moves in the wind to the east and to the west, between the sun and the earth."

And the grass looked up, and for the first time beheld the tree. And it said in its heart, "Why, behold, there is a larger grass than myself."

And the grass was silent.

The Pomegranates

There was once a man who had many pomegranate trees in his orchard. And for many an autumn he would put his pomegranates on silvery trays outside of his dwelling, and upon the trays he would place signs upon which he himself had written, "Take one for aught. You are welcome."

But people passed by and no one took of the fruit.

Then the man bethought him, and one autumn he placed no pomegranates on silvery trays outside of his dwelling, but he raised this sign in large lettering: "Here we have the best pomegranates in the land, but we sell them for more silver than any other pomegranates."

And now behold, all the men and women of the neighborhood came rushing to buy.

God and Many Gods

In the city of Kilafis a sophist stood on the steps of the Temple and preached many gods. And the people said in their hearts, "We know all this. Do they not live with us and follow us wherever we go?"

Not long after, another man stood in the market place and spoke unto the people and said, "There is no god." And many who heard him were glad of his tidings, for they were afraid of gods.

And upon another day there came a man of great eloquence, and he said, "There is but one God." And now the people were dismayed for in their hearts they feared the judgment of one God more than that of many gods.

That same season there came yet another man, and he said to the people, "There are three gods, and they dwell upon the wind as one, and they have a vast and gracious mother who is also their mate and their sister."

Then everyone was comforted, for they said in their secret, "three gods in one must needs disagree over our failings, and besides, their gracious mother will surely be an advocate for us poor weaklings."

Yet even to this day there are those in the city of Kilafis who wrangle and argue with each other about many gods and no god, and one god and three gods in one, and a gracious mother of gods.

She Who Was Deaf

Once there lived a rich man who had a young wife, and she was stone deaf.

And upon a morning when they were breaking their feast, she spoke to him and she said, "Yesterday I visited the market place, and there were exhibited silken raiment from Damascus, and coverchiefs from India, necklaces from Persia, and bracelets from Yamman. It seems that the caravans had but just brought these things to our city. And now behold me, in rags, yet the wife of a rich man. I would have some of those beautiful things."

The husband, still busy with his morning coffee said, "My dear, there is no reason why you should not go down to the Street and buy all that your heart may desire."

And the deaf wife said, "'No!' You always say, 'No, no.' Must I needs appear in tatters among our friends to shame your wealth and my people?"

And the husband said, "I did not say, 'No.' You may go forth freely to the market place and purchase the most beautiful apparel and jewels that have come to our city."

But again the wife mis-read his words, and she replied, "Of all rich men you are the most miserly. You would deny me everything of beauty and loveliness, while other women of my age walk the gardens of the city clothed in rich raiment."

And she began to weep. And as her tears fell upon her breast she cried out again, "You always say, 'Nay, nay' to me when I desire a garment or a jewel."

Then the husband was moved, and he stood up and took out of his purse a handful of gold and placed it before her, saying in a kindly voice, "Go down to the market place, my dear, and buy all that you will."

From that day onward the deaf young wife, whenever she desired anything, would appear before her husband with a pearly tear in her eye, and he in silence would take out a handful of gold and place it in her lap.

Now, it changed that the young woman fell in love with a youth whose habit it was to make long journeys. And whenever he was away she would sit in her casement and weep.

When her husband found her thus weeping, he would say in his heart, "There must be some new caravan, and some silken garments and rare jewels in the Street."

And he would take a handful of gold and place it before her.

The Quest

A thousand years ago two philosophers met on a slope of Lebanon, and one said to the other, "Where goest thou?"

And the other answered, "I am seeking after the fountain of youth which I know dwells out among these hills. I have found writings which tell of that fountain flowering toward the sun. And you, what are you seeking?"

The first man answered, "I am seeking after the mystery of death."

Then each of the two philosophers conceived that the other was lacking in his great science, and they began to wrangle, and to accuse each other of spiritual blindness.

Now while the two philosophers were loud upon the wind, a stranger, a man who was deemed a simpleton in his own village, passed by, and when he heard the two in hot dispute, he stood awhile and listened to their argument.

Then he came near to them and said, "My good men, it seems that you both really belong to the same school of philosophy, and that you are speaking of the same thing, only you speak in different words. One of you is seeks the fountain of youth, and the other seeks the mystery of death. Yet indeed they are but one, and as they dwell in you both."

Then the stranger turned away saying, "Farewell sages." And as he departed he laughed a patient laughter.

The two philosophers looked at each other in silence for a moment, and then they laughed also. And one of them said, "Well now, shall we not walk and seek together."

The Scepter

Said a king to his wife, "Madame, you are not truly a queen. You are too vulgar and ungracious to be my mate."

Said his wife, "Sir, you deem yourself king, but indeed you are only a poor soundling."

Now these words angered the king, and he took his scepter with his hand, and struck the queen upon her forehead with his golden scepter.

At that moment the lord chamberlain entered, and he said, "Well, well, Majesty! That scepter was fashioned by the greatest artist of the land. Alas! Some day you and the queen shall be forgotten, but this scepter shall be kept, a thing of beauty from generation to generation. And now that you have drawn blood from her Majesty's head, Sire, the scepter shall be the more considered and remembered."

The Path

There lived among the hills a woman and her son, and he was her first-born and her only child.

And the boy died of a fever whilst the physician stood by.

The mother was distraught with sorrow, and she cried to the physician and besought him saying, "Tell me, tell me, what was it that made quiet his striving and silent his song?"

And the physician said, "It was the fever."

And the mother said, "What is the fever?"

And the physician answered, "I cannot explain it. It is a thing infinitely small that visits the body, and we cannot see it with the human eye."

Then the physician left her. And she kept repeating to herself, "Something infinitely small. We cannot see it with our human eye."

And at evening the priest came to console her. And she wept and she cried out saying, "Oh, why have I lost my son, my only son, my first-born?"

And the priest answered, "My child, it is the will of God."

And the woman said, "What is God and where is God? I would see God that I may tear my bosom before Him, and pour the blood of my heart at His feet. Tell me where I shall find Him."

And the priest said, ""God is infinitely vast. He is not to be seen with our human eye."

Then the woman cried out, "The infinitely small has slain my son through the will of the infinitely great! Then what are we? What are we?"

At that moment the woman's mother came into the room with the shroud for the dead boy, and she heard the words of the priest and also her daughter's cry. And she laid down the shroud, and took her daughter's hand in her own hand, and she said, "My daughter, we ourselves are the infinitely small and the infinitely great; and we are the path between the two."

The Whale and the Butterfly

Once on an evening a man and a woman found themselves together in a stagecoach. They had met before.

The man was a poet, and as he sat beside the woman he sought to amuse her with stories, some that were of his own weaving, and some that were not his own.

But even while he was speaking the lady went to sleep. Then suddenly the coach lurched, and she awoke, and she said, "I admire your interpretation of the story of Jonah and the whale."

And the poet said, "But Madame, I have been telling you a story of mine own about a butterfly and a white rose, and how they behaved the one to the other!"

Peace Contagious

One branch in bloom said to his neighboring branch, "This is a dull and empty day." And the other branch answered, "It is indeed empty and dull."

At that moment a sparrow alighted on one of the branches, and the another sparrow, nearby.

And one of the sparrows chirped and said, "My mate has left me."

And the other sparrow cried, "My mate has also gone, and she will not return. And what care I?"

Then the two birds began to twitter and scold, and soon they were fighting and making harsh noise upon the air.

All of a sudden two other sparrows came sailing from the sky, and they sat quietly beside the restless two. And there was calm, and there was peace.

Then the four flew away together in pairs.

And the first branch said to his neighboring branch, "That was a mighty zig-zag of sound."

And the other branch answered, "Call it what you will, it is now both peaceful and spacious. And if the upper air makes peace it seems to me that those who dwell in the lower might make peace also. Will you not wave in the wind a little nearer to me?"

And the first branch said, "Oh, perchance, for peace' sake, ere the Spring is over."

And then he waved himself with the strong wind to embrace her.

Seventy

The poet youth said to the princess, "I love you." And the princess answered, "And I love you too, my child."

"But I am not your child. I am a man and I love you."

And she said, "I am the mother of sons and daughters, and they are fathers and mothers of sons and daughters; and one of the sons of my sons is older than you."

And the poet youth said, "But I love you."

It was not long after that the princess died. But ere her last breath was received again by the greater breath of earth, she said within her soul, "My beloved, mine only son, my youth-poet, it may yet be that some day we shall meet again, and I shall not be seventy."

Finding God

Two men were walking in the valley, and one man pointed with his finger toward the mountain side, and said, "See you that hermitage? There lives a man who has long divorced the world. He seeks but after God, and naught else upon this earth."

And the other man said, "He shall not find God until he leaves his hermitage, and the aloneness of his hermitage, and returns to our world, to share our joy and pain, to dance with our dancers at the wedding feast, and to weep with those who weep around the coffins of our dead."

And the other man was convinced in his heart, though in spite of his conviction he answered, "I agree with all that you say, yet I believe the hermit is a good man. And it may it not well be that one good man by his absence does better than the seeming goodness of these many men?"

The River

In the valley of Kadisha where the mighty river flows, two little streams met and spoke to one another.

One stream said, "How came you, my friend, and how was your path?"

And the other answered, "My path was most encumbered. The wheel of the mill was broken, and the master farmer who used to conduct me from my channel to his plants, is dead. I struggled down oozing with the filth of laziness in the sun. But how was your path, my brother?"

And the other stream answered and said, "Mine was a different path. I came down the hills among fragrant flowers and shy willows; men and women drank of me with silvery cups, and little children paddled their rosy feet at my edges, and there was laughter all about me, and there were sweet songs. What a pity that your path was not so happy."

At that moment the river spoke with a loud voice and said, "Come in, come in, we are going to the sea. Come in, come in, speak no more. Be with me now. We are going to the sea. Come in, come in, for in me you shall forget you wanderings, sad or gay. Come in, come in. And you and I will forget all our ways when we reach the heart of our mother the sea."

The Two Hunters

Upon a day in May, Joy and Sorrow met beside a lake. They greeted one another, and they sat down near the quiet waters and conversed.

Joy spoke of the beauty which is upon the earth, and the daily wonder of life in the forest and among the hills, and of the songs heard at dawn and eventide.

And Sorrow spoke, and agreed with all that Joy had said; for Sorrow knew the magic of the hour and the beauty thereof. And Sorrow was eloquent when he spoke of May in the fields and among the hills.

And Joy and Sorrow talked long together, and they agreed upon all things of which they knew.

Now there passed by on the other side of the lake two hunters. And as they looked across the water one of them said, "I wonder who are those two persons?" And the other said, "Did you say two? I see only one."

The first hunter said, "But there are two." And the second said, "There is only one that I can see, and the reflection in the lake is only one."

"Nay, there are two," said the first hunter, "and the reflection in the still water is of two persons."

But the second man said again, "Only one do I see." And again the other said, "But I see two so plainly."

And even unto this day one hunter says that the other sees double; while the other says, "My friend is somewhat blind."

The Other Wanderer

Once on a time I met another man of the roads. He too was a little mad, and thus spoke to me:

"I am a wanderer. Oftentimes it seems that I walk the earth among pygmies. And because my head is seventy cubits farther from the earth than theirs, it creates higher and freer thoughts.

"But in truth I walk not among men but above them, and all they can see of me is my footprints in their open fields.

"And often have I heard them discuss and disagree over the shape and size of my footprints. For there are some who say, 'These are the tracks of a mammoth that roamed the earth in the far past.' And others say, 'Nay, these are places where meteors have fallen from the distant stars.'

"But you, my friend, you know full well that they are naught save the footprints of a wanderer."

Made in the USA
Coppell, TX
03 December 2019

12338137R00095